A Charmed Life
A Memoir

By

José María Lacambra Loizu

A Charmed Life
A Memoir

iUniverse books may be ordered through booksellers or by contacting:

iUniverse
1663 Liberty Drive
Bloomington, IN 47403
www.iuniverse.com
1-800-Authors (1-800-288-4677)

ISBN: 978-1-4697-9294-1 (sc)
ISBN: 978-1-4697-9295-8 (e)

Printed in the United States of America

iUniverse rev. date: 4/10/2012

Foreword

One reaches that stage in life when his retrospective view becomes longer than the vistas lying before him. Even though one should avoid nostalgic reminiscences for their own sake, repression of the past invariably spawns a present bereft of direction, foolishly locking out the experience of one's past. And so, taking Spinoza at his word, I will, in what follows, feign to ignore history in hopes of having to relive it, however vicariously.

How better to conjure the evanescent than by evoking half-forgotten poems, limpid smells, or haunting strains of younger, more vibrant yesterdays? Reminiscing brings the liveliest of pleasures, when inchoate and amorphous recollections bubble up, changing to music what was only strain. But this occurs only when one's guard is down, when one's mind suddenly stirs to cognizance and, as if ashamed of having forgotten some joyous incident of long ago, bursts out in tears, laughing at his own forgetfulness and, in so doing, becomes young again.

JML

Winter Park, January 2012

Table of Contents

Chapter	1	The Early Years	1
"	2	War	15
"	3	The Homeward Passage	41
"	4	Pamplona	63
"	5	Bilbao	77
"	6	Africa	91
"	7	Paris	111
"	8	The Dawning	121
"	9	Coming to the States	129
"	10	College	139
"	11	Graduate School	163
"	12	Return of the Native	183
"	13	Orlando	191
"	14	Sundowning Years	213
"	15	*Querencia*	231

You can never say something meaningful by
accumulating absurdities in your notebook…
Facts don't exist until man puts into them
something of his own, a bit of free human genius,
of myth.

Dr. Zhivago
Boris Pasternak

Chapter 1

The Early Years

"Times lose no time nor do they roll by idly but plant
things in the mind and heal the wounds with patches
of old delights."

The Confessions
St. Augustine

It always gave me an odd feeling to realize that my birthplace
was not my motherland. I attribute that oddity to my parents' nostalgic
stories of their far-away homeland which impressed upon me, early on,
my own notions of roots. Ever since I can remember, their native land
had always been my mother country, their language my native tongue.
Although I was, by happenstance, born in the tropics, my earliest dreams
were of a far-away land I'd never actually seen but already knew and
loved, a land of craggy mountains, draped in summer green and winter
snows, with white sheep and blond Pyrenean cattle grazing along its
vales and upland greens, a land peopled by strong men and handsome
women, a patch of land my ancestors had inhabited since time
immemorial, where Basque, a tongue as ancient as their Cro-Magnon
forebears, was still spoken. Those were roots not easily ignored.

It was by a stroke of good fortune that my father, Luis, then a
young cabinetmaker apprentice in Elizondo, deep in the Basque
mountain country, was offered a job with a large Spanish conglomerate
in the Philippines. Part of its allure were its many commercial interests,
like gold mines, shipping, paint factories, distilleries, and, most
profitable of all, sugarcane plantations and sugar mills. Dad's earnest
demeanor, hard work ethic and deep-seated sense of honor led to his
inevitable rise in the Firm's administrative ladder, earning him, after

1

only a few years in the job, an executive position in the corporation's coveted sugar business. Being one of the richest sugar-producing islands in the Philippine archipelago, he was assigned to the Company's Iloilo office in Panay, the westernmost of the Visayan Island group, to head up the corporation's burgeoning sugar operations.

A few years into his job, while on a sabbatical leave in Spain, he heard of the Hotel Loizu, a quaint little inn in Burguete, a whitewashed, postage stamp-sized town fast by the Pyrenean foothills, in the hinterlands of the ancient Basque Kingdom of Navarre. Though drawn to the inn's picturesque surroundings and excellent fare, his interest was piqued by the buzz about five handsome young women living there, helping their widowed mother run the family hotel.

It didn't take long for him to fall head over heels in love with Laura, the next-to-youngest and liveliest of the Loizu brood. For her, too, it must have been love at first sight for, though already engaged to a military officer stationed in town, she did not hesitate to accept the engagement ring the dashing young *Filipino* offered her one moonlit night, while dancing in the square of the nearby town of Garralda during fiestas. Here was, she must have mused, this dashing young man dropping in from out of the blue, driving his own Morris Minor - a luxury only the well-off could afford those days - talking about an intriguing job in some exotic land halfway around the world. It all sounded so romantic! Having learned French in a finishing school across the border, she could tell a true *coup de foudre,* when one struck.

His vacations coming to an end, there was little time for the usual protracted courting niceties. They married shortly after having met and took off on their honeymoon to sunny southern Spain. The happy interlude left barely enough time to board the first ship scheduled to sail for the Philippines, with no time for even one last family farewell. He was 35 then, she only 19. It would be nineteen years before she'd see her family again.

Boarding an Orient-bound steamship in Barcelona, she was all a-tingle in anticipation of discovering an exotic new land on the other side of the world. The trip to the Far East must have been both daunting and exhilarating. There was a whole new world to discover for someone who'd never ventured farther away from home than St. Jean de Pied Port, the little French town across the border, where she'd attended finishing school. Crossing the Suez Canal, braving the irascible Indian Ocean, negotiating the straits of Malacca and sailing finally into Manila Bay took slightly over a month. From there, the final short hop to Iloilo, capital of the southern island of Panay, must have been a blessing after all those endless sea-sick weeks.

They settled in a small cottage by the sea on General Hughes Avenue. Dad returned to his business duties and his meetings while Mom kept house, all the time meeting worldly-wise lady friends at the Casino Español, the Spanish watering hole. Her new acquaintances were

all too happy to take the young, charmingly-naïve country girl from the Old Country under their wing to teach her the ropes and show her the finer points of life in the old Spanish colony. Although the Americans had taken over the administration of the islands decades earlier, Spain's old traditions and imperial splendor died slowly and the few Spanish stragglers remaining behind were determined to draw out the niceties and little glories of *la belle époque* as best they could.

It was a brand spanking new world for the young émigré, dressing up to the nines on endless parties and enchanting soirées, meeting important people and hosting visiting dignitaries. But motherhood was soon to cut into all those worldly activities and occupy her undivided attention. Her four children came in fairly rapid succession. Following her Basque country's religious tradition, all of her progeny's names had "Mary" appended to them. Mari Blanca came first, a strong-willed, auburn-haired girl who inherited her father's deep-set brown eyes and resolute look. Two years later came José Mari, the first of two boys, this one a broad-browed, independent spirit who also favored his father's features. Luis Mari, the younger brother, had a pliant character and easy-going disposition, was blonde and blue-eyed like his maternal grandfather Loizu. Being only two years apart, the brothers' relationship was sprinkled with episodes of both camaraderie and sibling rivalry. Maria Mercedes, the youngest, came four years later. She was nicknamed *Maite*, Basque for "beloved," a sentiment she inspired in almost everyone who got to meet her. Slight and feminine, she inherited her mother's gentle, graceful ways and calm, easygoing temperament.

As Dad's job grew in importance, the family moved from the unpretentious cottage on Hughes Ave. to a grand old Spanish colonial home on Calle Progreso. Located not far from the first bend in the Iloilo River, the two-storied structure had a certain seigniorial air about it, with ample accommodation for the family and adjoining quarters for the help.

The colonial residence soon became our happy home. It had enough alcoves and antechambers and secret recesses to satisfy any child's wildest hide-and-seek fantasies. I still remember the scroll-molded stairway sweeping grandly up to the reception hall, where countless introductions were made and appointments kept. That was about 1935, the time Dad was named Spain's Honorary Consul in town.

I remember racing Luis down the stairway's broad mahogany handrail, the winner being the first to touch our secret home base, the now-shiny right nipple of one of the bronze Naiads standing pert guard at the bottom of the scrolled sweep. I used to win most of those races, rationalizing that older brothers had their privileges. I sometimes felt a  little guilty about the false starts and also a little humbled by the thought that, deep down, I knew my kid brother's heart contained more gold than mine. He must have been five when Mom found him frantically blowing air under the door of a closet where I'd accidentally locked myself, fearing I was suffocating inside. But we were too close in years to let the odd squishy moments

4

interfere with the roughhousing. The Yaya doled out punishment with great abandon but the nanny's ear-boxing and pinching merely brought on the giggles. Once, during the hallowed quiet of Dad's half hour siesta, we were at it as usual, snapping wet towels at one another, crashing toy cars against each other's, or engaging in paper airplane fly-offs from our bedroom window, oblivious of the litter we were leaving in the garden below. I'll never forget the afternoon we were raucously laughing as we shook talcum powder and splashed water at each other, when Dad stormed into the bedroom to settle interrupted siesta accounts. His slipping on the pasty talcum goop, trying to extricate us from under the beds, didn't help matters any.

One of my earliest recollections of that colonial residence was the huge mango tree growing in the middle of the large enclosed garden, from whose branches I'd swing, pretending to be the ape-man in the movies. I remember asking Mari Blanca to fashion a Tarzan-like loincloth for me, with which to modestly swing between its tree limbs. Wondering aloud one day about the mango tree's barrenness, Eusebio, the older of the two menservants, lit a small fire under it, explaining that its barrenness merely needed a little "smoking out." The quaint procedure worked like a charm because it started producing copious crops of delicious mangoes.

I also remember the circular pond with its own little fountain sitting in the middle of the patio, where we would take dips to cool off in the muggy tropical weather. Hanging all around the patio were mother's cherished orchids, lovingly nestled in individual coconut husks, adding a touch of color to the all-pervading tropical green. The orchids seldom needed watering in the rainy season, when it poured torrentially for months on end.

There was a notable increase in the number of household servants when we moved to the new residence. There were two *yayas*, or nurses; Esperanza, the girls' governess, and the short, inappropriately-named Consolación, who tried mightily to keep us boys under control. Eusebio and Juan, the menservants, handled the heavy chores of cleaning house and serving at table. They also doubled as trackers whenever Luis and I evaded our yaya.

5

Cirilo, the chauffeur of the shiny family Desoto, had the most interesting job of that motley crew. He'd grow discomfited every time we smudged the pristine sheen off his pampered car. One day, Esperanza's flirtations with him landed her with child, prompting Mom to lower the boom on them; her ultimatum was simple enough: either marry or leave. Averse to the threatened consequence, they opted for the more honorable option.

Even at his advanced age, Angel, the cantankerous cook, never hesitated to chase Luis and me out of the kitchen whenever he surprised us snitching his French fries or whittling wood with his painstakingly sharpened paring knives. In wide-eyed wonderment, we'd watch him force a spoonful of brandy down a chicken's gullet minutes before wringing its neck, bafflingly explaining that the method "gave it character."

The help's dining room adjoined the kitchen. I would drop in on them during their noon repast to sample their native delicacies. I was particularly fond of their balls of sticky-rice, lathered in *guinamús,* a pungent baby shrimp paste, their *lumpiâ* vegetable soup, and their sweet *poto bonbón* rice cakes. On festive occasions, I'd even sneak a sip of *tubâ,* their fermented coconut juice. My ensuing giddiness invariably drew giggles from the congregation. Foremost in my bag of memories of those kitchen incursions, however, was the delicious taste of Peking duck, which Dad's Chinese friends presented him in appreciation for some business favor. He'd promptly send the delicacy to the kitchen, untouched. For some misplaced sense of chauvinism, he adamantly refused to savor exotic oriental dishes, insisting that only European fare be served at his table.

The laundress and the gardener brought up the rear of the motley crew. The latter constantly grumbled about our paper airplanes littering his yard, while puzzling over the suspicious smell of ammonia around his wilted *gumamela* hibiscuses. The flowers happened to grow directly under our bedroom window, through whose bottom grill Luis and I relieved ourselves at night to avoid walking the few paces to the adjoining bathroom.

The laundress, who was all business and seldom cracked a smile, spent her days ironing clothes in the garage. She used an ancient coal-burning iron, whose smoky emanations must have exacerbated her innate ill-temper. She owned a short, wicked-looking knife which she'd whip out from under her *sarong* at the slightest provocation, like the time Luis and I accidentally splattered mud on some bed sheets hanging out to dry in the sun. We spent little time rushing for the exits when that threat loomed.

Belonging to a select Spanish colonial society, our parents were members of the Casino Español and several other local upper-crust societies, like the Golf Country Club and sundry other social clubs, where they'd rub elbows with Spanish, American and English friends. How Dad communicated with his foreign friends never ceased to intrigue me.

Being a natural athlete, Dad excelled at practically every sport he practiced, especially handball, bowling, tennis and golf. Mom enjoyed playing Mahjong with her friends, all of whom refused to learn Visayâ, the local dialect, lest it dull their sense of superiority, a studied aloofness not unlike the English in their British Raj. Mom, however, soon tired of being a golf widow and eventually picked up badminton and golf, winning not a few trophies of her own, in the process. I still remember the large display case in the living room, filled to overflowing with both their trophies. It didn't take her long to learn English, either. Dad, on the other hand, insisted on limiting his verbal communications to his native tongue. "Let them learn Spanish," he'd retort huffily whenever anyone suggested he learn English, the up-and-coming *lingua franca* in the islands.

My parents hosted frequent gala affairs, with important visitors and foreign dignitaries like visiting ambassadors and famous concert pianists. There were also renowned visiting athletes, like Henri Lacoste, the French tennis champion, and Gene Sarazen, the American golfer in the mid thirties, then on a world exhibition tour, shortly after winning his Grand Slam. Either by sheer luck or pure merit, Dad beat him at his own game one day at his Country Club. Jealous of his improbable victory, some of his golf buddies claimed Sarazen must have been indisposed that day. Much to their chagrin, the feat was prominently splattered in the local papers, all that next week. I was too young to play golf but whenever Dad took me along to the Country Club, I remember holding my breath as Cirilo drove us past the local Leprosarium, believing I was, thus, avoiding contracting the dread disease.

Dad also enjoyed hunting big and small game, frequently filling our larder with wild boar and a variety of native fowl; *agachonas*, a variety of native snipe, stick in my mind. In the glow of the ensuing feast, Mom would revert to her French and utter phrases like "*Comme la vie est belle[1]*!" As well she should; transplanted from a sleepy little mountain village in the Pyrenees to the dazzling big time of High Society in the Tropics must have been like dying and going to heaven

We quickly made friends with boys our age when we moved to the new neighborhood. I became particularly close to Lawson Davies and Jesus Jimenez, the former a son of a Scottish Engineer, the latter a Bank President's son. Because one-upmanship was the name of the game those days, Lawson's father one day acquired a TV set that simply hissed its white noise at us whenever turned on, the first Television broadcast in the islands still years away. Not to be bested, Jesus' father acquired an air conditioner from Sears Roebuck that was limited to blowing warm air when turned on, it being years before Freon became available in the islands.

Much to our yayas' chagrin, my brother and I were always on delinquent errands such as raiding some neighbor's guava orchard or dropping firecrackers behind some unsuspecting old lady ambling by. Our parents organized frequent neighborhood parties which, of course, we children had to attend. I remember having to wear a white sailor suit

---

[1] Many years later and with her inhibitions down, she'd add: "*"..et les enfants si facile a faire, surtout aux pères.*"

with a blue-striped collar on those festive occasions, complete with an outsized bowtie and a sailor's cap, all of which I cordially detested. I must have been developing a sense of the ridiculous even at that early age.

On turning five, my brother and I were enrolled in Colegio San Agustin, a school run by Spanish friars, while our sisters were sent to Colegio de la Asunción, a nun-run private school. English was the official language in both schools, and since we spoke Spanish at home, English in school, and Visayâ - the local dialect –with the help and with native schoolmates, we effortlessly turned trilingual at an early age.

Second Grade class picture (1938), Colegio San Agustin, Iloilo. Author, then aged 7, is in second row, far right.

Constantly encouraged by Dad, we thrived at our academic endeavors, consistently winning the Valedictorian award in our respective classes at the end of each school year, an award which pleased our parents immeasurably.

Fisticuffs those days were an almost daily occurrence during recess at school. Consequently, developing boxing dexterity came fairly naturally. As a Christmas gift one year, Dad gave us a pair of boxing gloves he'd ordered from Sears & Roebuck to cut down on sibling nosebleeds. Although boxing was the sport of choice in school, we also participated in team sports such as soccer, basketball, and volleyball. Other less demanding pastimes during recess included marbles, slingshot contests, top-splitting and spider-fighting competitions.

The latter was the most exciting. We'd collect different types of spiders from the bushes in our garden, blow on them in the cup of our hands to calm them enough so we could stash them away in empty matchboxes. During recess at school, we'd challenge our prize spiders against the other kids'. Placing them at each end of a stripped palm leaf rib, we'd watch them approach each other warily, prodding them gently until they tangled. Each spider fought with a distinct style until one of them overcame the other. The *Pulahan's* (red) technique consisted in immobilizing its opponent by wrapping it's legs up in the sticky web it drew from its rear end at a blurring speed. White and smaller in size, the *King* variety used its neurotoxin bite to paralyze its opponent. The defeated spider was deposited in the winner's matchbox, there to serve as the spider's weekly sustenance.

When school vacations started at the end of March, the family would sail off to Manila, where we rented a car that took us to the lovely summer resort city of Baguio, in the Luzon highlands. It was an attractive little town, not unlike a fabled Philippine Shangri-La. The cottage we rented was neat and clean, perched atop a hill in the middle of a pine forest. I can still smell the sweet, pungent scent of pine resin and the needle-covered slopes down which Luis and I would mirthfully slide-race. One of the delightful advantages of living in a cooler climate was not sleeping under mosquito nets, a blessing understandable only to unwary sleepers in the tropics who would wake up in the morning to find an arm or a cheek riddled with mosquito bites for having inadvertently rested them against the net while asleep.

After breakfast, our yayas would take us down to the skating rink in Burnham Park, under the shadows of the classy Pines Hotel. On other occasions they'd make us walk endless miles up and down steep mountain trails, wearing us out to the point of tears. During some of those walks we'd amble past the fancy American Camp John Hay golf course. On other occasions, we'd walk to the monastery on top of Dominican Hill, to watch Dad play handball with his Basque friar friends.

Sometimes, during some of those interminable walks, we'd come across a small troop of swarthy, native *Igorrotes,* loaded down with beautifully-carved wooden statuettes they'd hawk in the town's tourist market. In a sinister undertone, our yayas confided that this particular tribe was known for fattening their dogs during the year only to slaughter and consume them on their yearly festival atop one of the nearby mountains. We were understandably shaken by the story, which was, I suspect, why the yayas shared the gruesome tidbit, in the first place.

During some of those vacations, the Iturraldes would join us in our Baguio cottage. Being Basque like my parents, they were close acquaintances. Mr. Iturralde's short stature earned him the unkind nickname of "*el peque,*" or "shorty", a moniker he didn't seem to greatly mind. He was a prissy little man, always absorbed with the care and luster of his nails.

Mrs. Iturralde, on the other hand, was tall, good-looking and born to mischief. She once gave Luis and me a pair of Conde de Güell cigars, on condition we smoke them down in the basement so the others wouldn't find out. They had to drag us out of there half an hour later,

11

vomiting and retching uncontrollably. The experience cured us of cigars for life. For some reason, that incident always reminds me of Dad's forcing us to swallow a spoonful of Castor Oil whenever we came down with a fever, regardless of provenance. Our abhorrence for the laxative was so strident that he tried diluting its revolting taste by mixing it in a glass of orange juice, coffee, and, once, even beer! We were well into our twenties before we got over our revulsion for those drinks. I believe psychologists call it "repression by association", or something like that.

I remember undergoing a tonsillectomy on one of those Baguio vacations, not because I needed one but simply because it was fashionable those days. I woke up gagging from the administered ether anesthetic. Carmen Iturralde came to the rescue when she burst into the recovery room with a large ice cream cone. I was in the process of devouring it when the nun in charge of the ward came into the room, yanked the cone from my hands and proceeded to rebuke Mrs. Iturralde for having broken some hospital rule. Unimpressed, Mrs. Iturralde simply smiled benignly at her tormentor, offered no excuses and went out for another ice cream cone.

Although the Baguio vacations were, by themselves, unforgettable, there were other equally memorable interludes back in Iloilo, during the school year. On rare occasions, Dad would take me along on his inspection tours of different sugar plantations. It was on one such trip to Sara Ajuy that, on a dare, I shot a heron through the neck with a .22 caliber rifle someone lent me. We happened to be sailing up river on a small launch at the time, so it amounted to hitting a moving target. I was as impressed by my fluky marksmanship as was everybody else.

I took my first airplane ride on one of those inspection outings to the neighboring island of Negros. The flight on the single-engine, six-passenger Stimson, was bumpy and exciting, but otherwise uneventful. A subsequent, even more thrilling flight was on a small Sikorsky seaplane that took off from the beach off the small airport near Fort San

12

Pedro. I rode my first horse at the La Carlota sugar plantation in the nearby island of Negros. I vividly remember Dad surreptitiously riding up from behind and slapping my mount to a startled gallop. I was so thrilled by the jolt that I couldn't stop spurring it myself after that, galloping for the rest of that unforgettable day.

Chapter 2

WAR

"If it be peace we crave, as so we cry,
Let there be tumult first, that it may die."

"Yet these Eleven"
Jac Chambliss

Life took a turn for the worse on December 8, 1941, when the Japanese bombed Pearl Harbor[2]. Sensing the imminence of a Japanese invasion of the islands, schools closed and all the help absconded to their homes in the hill country. Dad moved the family to Molo, a town on the suburbs of Iloilo. Ten days later, back in town for a haircut, I witnessed the first Japanese air-raid firsthand. In less than fifteen minutes, Japanese dive bombers destroyed the city's wharf area, killing 50 civilians in the process. Several of the casualties were classmates of mine who happened to live in the neighborhood. The incident prompted Dad to move the family farther away from town, this time to Igbarás, a sleepy little town in the inland foothills, some 30 miles distant.

Life in the country was an eye-opener for an eleven-year old. With no schoolwork to worry about and free to roam, my brother and I quickly reverted to our usual devilment, carrying on as if we owned the

---

[2] In the Philippines, the infamous event took place one calendar day later than in the States due to the International dateline

sleepy little town. We rode horses and carabao-pulled sleds, spent endless hours cavorting in the river, and played one baseball game after another with other refugee kids in the plaza near home.

Paking, an altar boy in the local church, was given charge of a thoroughbred racehorse which its owner had shipped to the countryside for safety. Much to my surprise and delight, Paking let me ride the brute one day. I noticed, only too late, that there was no way of braking the fiery beast while ineffectively pulling on home-made reins fashioned out of pliant strips of old rubber tires. The horse's speed literally took my breath away. Halfway into my first run, the fiery stallion suddenly slowed down to a trot to better sniff the scent of an Arabian mare in heat, which my friend Sandro Aboitiz happened to be riding nearby. Soon the chase was on. Chickens flew; pigs squealed out of the way; children gawked at the two horses racing through town at a mad gallop. Aware of the peril he was in, Sandro had the presence of mind to steer his mount into a farmer's barn and quickly slam the door shut behind him. My stallion came to an abrupt halt, snorting disconsolately.

The beehive episode took place soon after. One day, armed with slingshots, our gang of refugee kids lined up some twenty paces from a beehive hanging placidly from a tree limb on the outskirts of town. No sooner had we dropped the hive with a telling volley than a swarm of angry bees zeroed in on the culprits. We had just enough time to make it to the river, diving into it to evade the threatening cloud. That wasn't good enough; we got thoroughly stung every time we surfaced for air. There wasn't enough Mentholatum in the medicine cabinet at the town infirmary that afternoon to soothe the myriad beestings on our heads and shoulders.

The crazed carabao incident was the highlight of our delinquent forays in Igbarás. A kindly neighborhood farmer let us ride the wooden sled drawn by his tame carabao up and down the nearby hills. Impatient with its plodding gait, Luis and I prodded the beast's genitals with a stick in an attempt to speed it up a mite. Our poking served no purpose other than to instill a silent, lasting grudge in the beast's memory.

Mucking about the farmer's nipa hut during his lunch hour a few days later, we happened to notice his carabao tied to one of the hut's four stilts. Turning a lazy eyeball toward us, we noticed the beast's eyes suddenly turn red. After a few determined tugs at the stilt it was tied to, the crazed carabao managed to dislodge it from its moorings. As if in slow-motion, the hut came crashing down with a sickening thud, the dazed farmer and his family spilling out of the hut, screaming dementedly. The carabao, meanwhile, came charging after us, stilt still attached to the rope tied to its nostrils. We lit out fast and got home before the galumphing beast had a chance to overtake us. Having a decidedly superstitious bent, the townsfolk came abuzz with stories of the carabao's odd behavior, convinced an evil spirit had taken possession of the crazed beast.

One night, three months into our Igbarás interlude, the town was hit by a huge earthquake. The temblor was so violent it ejected me from the cot I was sleeping in. Waking up on the floor the next morning, the first thing I noticed, right at eyeball level, was a pair of scorpions climbing out of my sneakers. I got up from the floor with alacrity. Outside, the quake had caused a huge crack down the side of the town's colonial-era church, condemning it from further use. From then on, religious services were held in the plaza, out in the open.

In April of 1942, right after the Bataan and Corregidor strongholds in Manila Bay fell, the Japanese spread out to the other islands and landed on ours. After shooting up the local Constabulary, they took control of the town and promptly ordered us back to Iloilo. Being citizens of a neutral country, we were spared internment in the city's holding camp, where all of our American and English friends were momentarily confined, before being shipped to Manila's large concentration camp in Santo Tomas University.

Front view of Author's house in Iloilo.

The city we came back to had been devastated by fire, set, it was rumored, by its defenders' scorched-earth tactics during the invasion. Our grand old Colonial house had gone up in flames, along with several other houses in the neighborhood. We had to move into the Elizalde residence, a Colonial structure even larger and more imposing than ours that had somehow escaped the holocaust. It occupied a whole city block on Calle Real, the city's main thoroughfare. Overnight, running water and electricity had become things of the past and we had to make do with rain water and oil lamps for the duration. The running water shortage turned out to be a blessing in disguise for, as we later discovered the inmates of the local Leprosarium had absconded from their colony and gone skinny dipping in the city's nearby water reservoir. We suspected it may have been their way of evening things out with their erstwhile keepers.

There were other unfortunate incidents on our return to civilization; the Japanese commandeered our two cars, dad's .32 caliber pistol, and all our radios, not to mention every American textbook we owned. They attempted to sanitize these before returning them, by pasting over any picture depicting American scenes. Asia, they avowed, was for the Asiatics, from there on out.

The help started trickling back into town soon after. Floring and Juan Sumalakay were the latest additions to the staff. Floríng, an attractive young 18-year old, was barely popping out of her dress. Mom took care of that distraction by giving her less revealing garments. Juan was the sawed-off driver of the antediluvian WWI Ford sitting serenely on the mansion's basement, complete with solid rubber tires and a goose horn, looking very much like a displaced dinosaur. It was grounded there because gasoline was a scarce commodity, reserved only for the occupying forces. Hurt by the Japanese disdain for his relic, Juan pampered it shamelessly. He'd get wrapped around the axle every time Luis and I snuck past him to squeeze its goose horn, generating a noise sounding very much like someone passing wind.

Our schools remained closed for the time being. To keep us from getting underfoot, we were trundled off to a neighborhood school run by nuns of the Sagrado Corazon. From the beginning, mixing boys and girls in the same classes didn't seem like a good idea. Incidents of male delinquency became rife and, true to form, Jesus Jimenez emerged as the self-appointed ring leader of every misdemeanor. One of his first disrupting capers was the syncopated humming episode he talked us into, whereby our intermittent droning hums drove the teaching nun to distraction. Another of his dubious inspirations was the flying-flag lark. He showed us how to carefully stick a small, furled piece of white paper up a fly's rear end and keeping it in an empty matchbox until, at a whistled command in the middle of the next Religion lecture, we'd all simultaneously set our flies loose. The nun went literally unstable. We giggled uncontrollably, watching her attempting to swat several dozen droning peace flags from the classroom's airspace.

Boys raised such ruckus in that girls' school that the nuns simply begged our parents to send us back to our boys' school as soon as possible. We were only too happy to oblige when the transfer finally took place. I was eleven then and starting my first Year of High School. The new scholastic year came with such thorny subjects as Algebra, Science, and, oddest of all, Japanese language. I managed to learn the rudiments of Japanese despite despising it cordially. One of my favorite expressions was: *Wakarimasen*, which meant "I don't understand," a phrase I used liberally when confronted by some Japanese soldier shouting orders at me.

19

Fr. Fueyo, the erstwhile Latin teacher, was now in charge of teaching Japanese. He appeared greatly distressed by the barbaric language's lack of periphrastics, supines and subjunctives with which to torment his former Latin students. He blinked uncontrollably every time Jesus Jimenez slipped one of his barbarisms into the Japanese lyrics he was attempting to teach us. One of his more outrageous "inserts" went something like: *"A-a- ano kaode, bulî mo ma hapdî,"* a naughty spoonerism that only speakers of Visayâ understood and appreciated.

Mariano Uyeki, a former Japanese schoolmate who happened to be much older than any of us, was asked to join the Kempitai, the Japanese Military Police, shortly after they invaded the island. As payback for all the bullying he had been subjected to before the war, he delighted in exasperating his old classmates every chance he got. He'd strut around in his spanking new military uniform, complete with leggings, jackboots and a holstered .45. He'd force us to bow down low every time we walked past him as a sign of subservience, smacking us soundly whenever we failed to show the proper obeisance.

One afternoon, Uyeki happened to turn up as I was taking Iru, my pet fox terrier, out for a walk in nearby Plaza Libertad. Dogs seem to sense their master's likes and dislikes and, as if on cue, Iru started barking at him frenziedly. Feeling threatened by the unleashed yapping mutt, he pulled his bayonet from its scabbard and stabbed Iru through the back. My mind went blank when Iru died that evening. I was only twelve and too young for that kind of pain. I gasped for meaning, trying to fathom why anyone would take away life so wantonly. Mom and Dad tried to console me but their sympathy blew over me like dry wind on parched earth. My smoldering hatred for Uyeki and his occupation army grew boundlessly. It would, unfortunately, take several years to assuage the perpetrated wrong.

A few months after the Iru incident, Tancinco, a classmate of mine and I were walking home from school when Uyeki surprised him drawing on a street wall a P-38 shooting down a Japanese Zero.

Tancinco was promptly hustled to Kempitai Headquarters, bundled up in a sack and hung from a tree branch with a sign in Japanese apparently instructing any soldiers walking by to kick, maul or otherwise pummel the sack with the butt of his rifle. Tancinco never came back to school after that incident. It was only at the end of the war that I learned Uyeki had shot him through the head when they finally pulled him down from the tree branch. My once-meek Japanese classmate was eventually to pay dearly for that crime.[3]

Life turned harsher as the occupation dragged on. The funny money issued by the Japanese turned increasingly worthless. Angel, the cook, would go to market every morning with a wheelbarrow full of increasingly valueless occupation currency, returning several hours later with a scrawny chicken or a dozen sweet potatoes. Even those pitiful transactions came to a halt shortly after. People, who had reverted to the barter system, soon ran out of towels, bed sheets or old clothes with which to barter. Hunger gradually set in. Our meals were now limited to weasel-laden corn porridge for breakfast and lentil-like *mongo* beans with *tancong*, a nondescript green, for lunch and dinner.

---

[3] Being one of the few Japanese soldiers captured alive at the end of the war, he was judged guilty of murder by a military tribunal and summarily executed.

To celebrate one Christmas Eve dinner, Mom traded her diamond engagement ring for a dozen eggs. Sadly, they all turned out to be rotten, a poignant denouement not unlike something O'Henry would have written in one of his pathetic short stories. Mari Blanca developed Beriberi, a vitamin B deficiency, while Maite contracted *Bakukang*, a severe tropical infection, treatable only through cauterization. Luis and I fared somewhat better. We were thin and gaunt but not much the worse for wear. At 12, Luis began to outstrip me in height, miraculously bringing our fisticuffs to a gradual halt.

I joined the feeble ranks of acolytes in our Parish Church the day Jesus Jimenez and Angel Arana mentioned something about becoming altar boys. "The paten's an absolute sine-qua-non if you thwack the girls' Adam's apple hard enough with it during Communion," theorized Jesus, as further enticement. I soon discovered that the awkward maneuver did little to impress the girls.

Christmas time was the highlight of our altar boy year. The Parish priest sent the three of us out into the streets, dressed in our bright red robes and clean surplices, toting a crèche-sized figurine of the baby Jesus lying in a crib, for the townsfolk to kiss and render homage. We got to keep their monetary donations; it was the priest's way of compensating us for the meager allowance of the preceding year of Sundays.

"*Pax vobiscum!*" we'd cheerfully intone on entering people's homes. The family would line up to kiss the baby's protruding leg, its color now faded from the wiped slobber of a thousand previous kisses.

Our last two stops were the highlight of our religious outing. Standing conveniently across the street from each other, were the town's two houses of ill repute, one Filipino, the other Korean. Like skittish Crusaders, we drew forbidden pleasure from walking into the brothels, with religious sanction. Once inside, we'd gawk at the flimsily dressed prostitutes lolling about their living rooms, dressed in gaudy gowns and cheap trinkets.

Dim recollections of more modest days helped loosen the Filipino whores' purse strings. But being of an altogether different persuasion, the Korean prostitutes across the street didn't even understand the mythology at hand, looked on uncomprehendingly and ended up showing us the door. Jesus Jimenez vowed to convert the heathen the following year.

By the middle of 1944, American submarines started provisioning Filipino guerrillas with the latest automatic weaponry and ammunition. This enhanced firepower gradually forced the Japanese to fall back, first to defensive enclaves, then, finally, to a last ditch stand on the outskirts of town. The shortage of living quarters in the half-burned city was exacerbated by the sudden inflow of Japanese troops. We were now totally surrounded, living practically cheek-by-jowl with a detested enemy, and with literally nowhere to go. This, of course, had been our condition since the Japanese invaded the islands; we had been completely incommunicado with the outside world since then.

On the first week of September 1944, Colonel Ito, the Commander of the Occupation Army ordered us to vacate our home, claiming he needed it for his headquarters. On the afternoon of September 13, the day we were supposed to vacate the house, the first flight of American carrier warplanes came swooping down on the unsuspecting Japanese, carrying out the first American air raid on Iloilo. We were elated, despite being, on top of everything else, now on the receiving end of American bombs and bullets. The dire and untenable situation notwithstanding, we were thrilled by the thought that the hated Japanese were finally getting their comeuppance.

Much to students' delight, the war's crescendo prompted a second closing of all schools. Free to roam among, and inflict grief upon the despised occupation troops, our gang came up with several ingenious schemes which we were all too keen to carry out. More than two years had passed since the Iru and Tancinco incidents and yet their memory, silently kneaded, kept gurgling up, naggingly reminding me of unfulfilled promises. Though long nurtured, both the timing and the execution of their redress came unexpectedly.

The British-owned Hongkong & Shanghai National Bank was the unlikely grounds of our first open act of defiance against the Japanese Army. Shortly after the invasion, the Japanese had sealed all foreign banks and frozen their assets. Living next door to the British bank, Jesus Jimenez was inevitably recruited to help size up the job. The prospects of havoc made him salivate.

Luis, the Arana brothers and I followed him into the out-of-bounds bank one afternoon. Gaining access to the grounds, we broke into the abandoned building through a hesitant back door. Rummaging through the well appointed quarters in the mansion's second floor, Luis discovered a secret panel in one of the master bedroom's closets. Striking a match, we followed a dim passageway to a spiral staircase which dizzily wound down to the bank's main vault. Fashioning a torch out of strewn papers, we investigated the vault's clammy interior, noticing the warped surface and distorted hinges of the huge steel door; the Japanese had obviously been trying to unsuccessfully blow the safe open with explosive charges.

All we found inside its cavernous vault were packets of cancelled checks stacked high against the walls. Reading the checks by torchlight, I recognized Dad's signature in most of them. I also noticed that the fist-sized packets were flimsily bound by a thin, single-twist wire. It didn't take much imagination to recognize their potential for play ammunition, a suspicion quickly confirmed on watching one of the hurled packets disintegrate on contact with the wall, dramatically sun-bursting checks all over the place.

Lugging armfuls of them up the spiral stairway, we stockpiled them in different strategic locations around the house. The battle was soon joined. Blurred with flurries of strewn paper, the epic free-for-all waxed and waned all afternoon, with classic indecision. The noisy skirmishes raged up and down every floor, in and out of every room of that forbidden battleground. The marble floor of the bank's rotunda was littered with the debris of battle. It was a glorious long-to-be remembered mêlée. After running out of ammunition, we inspected the Bank's main offices. Figuring it was our patriotic duty to relieve the Japanese of their ill-got gains, we picked up as much office stationary and supplies as we could stuff under our shirts and in our pant pockets before leaving the premises.

A sentry was permanently posted at the Bank's front door after that raid, discouraging any further foray into the British bank. "That's one less soldier at the front," commented Luis wryly.

A second plan involved a moonlit assault on the Japanese launches anchored on the river wharf near home. After carefully timing the Japanese sentries' patrolling pattern along the quay, we hopped onto one launch after another, riffling through their ammunition cases. Filling our pockets with live .50-caliber machine gun bullets, we dropped our "loot" on the river on our way to the next launch. We were inordinately proud of our second sabotage activity.

Keen on more disruptive action, Luis and I planned a raid on a Japanese munitions depot near Fort San Pedro. In our spare time we had built a small sailboat out of a piece of galvanized tin roofing which we shaped into a hull. Wooden slats nailed to its midsection served both as structural support and seating arrangement, while bamboo poles attached to each end of two wooden beams served as outriggers. We painted the hull with generous coats of pitch to plug up its many old nail holes.

Its seaworthiness once ensured, we took her out on her maiden voyage and the intended raid. Rowing around the breakwaters, we slipped into the chosen cove undetected. Quietly wading ashore, we crouched behind the dunes, listening for telltale sounds. Craning our necks above the cattail reeds, we spotted a Japanese sentry soundly dozing on a stack of tarpaulin-covered boxes, rifle resting easy on his lap. He had not seen us. Disappointed by the aborted commando raid, we slipped out of the cove as quietly as we had sailed in, musing as we rowed away that the Japanese appeared increasingly edgy and that probably things weren't quite going their way any longer. It was now the third year of the war.

Late one afternoon, perched on our favorite observation post on our home's rooftop, Luis and I witnessed a dogfight between my very favorite warplane, the American three-bodied Lightning P-38,and an underpowered but feistier Japanese Zero. After some great aerobatics and exchanges of gunfire, the two airplanes disengaged and peeled off in opposite directions, either because of the onrushing darkness or because they were running low on fuel or ammunition. Though indecisive, that brief yet deadly spectacle was indelibly locked away in memory.

One of our more daring attempts at sabotage took place a few days after the dogfight show. Our gang happened to be playing Cowboys and Indians one afternoon on the deserted airfield by Fort San Pedro - where Dad and I had once taken off on the Stimson flight - when we saw a platoon of Japanese soldiers in the opposite end of the overgrown runway, unloading gasoline drums from several trucks, camouflaging them with dry cogon grass cuttings before departing.

After a brief council of war we decided to set fire to the dry cogon grass on our end of the field, knowing the fire would eventually reach the drums. After lighting the dry cogon grass in our end of the field and making sure the conflagration was proceeding as planned, we made tracks for home.

Half an hour later, in the middle of supper, we pretended surprise at the sudden roar of explosions in the distance. Dashing to the nearest window, we saw pillars of smoke rising above the general direction of the deserted airfield, Japanese fire trucks rushing to the scene, sirens wailing. We suspected it must have been the last of the fuel supply for their surviving rattletrap Zero because we never saw it fly again after that. They give medals for less brazen feats of sabotage, we smugly thought to ourselves.

Owning and operating a shortwave radio was an offense punishable by death those unsettled days. Yet Dad and several of his friends managed to squirrel away a radio, re-jiggering its snipped shortwave band condenser back to life and ingeniously recharging its battery with a bicycle-pedaled generator. Above the garbled static, they learned that on November of 1944, the Americans had landed in Leyte, just four islands east of ours, in the central Visayan group. Our excitement was boundless, hoping and praying that they'd keep moving west toward our island.

Because they were now much closer than their erstwhile carrier bases, their newly captured airfields meant more frequent and intensive American bombings. Dad ordered a sturdier air raid shelter built in our basement, where we'd congregate at the first sound of approaching airplanes. We learned to live through the rattling of teeth and popping of eardrums from the infernal 500-lb bombs dropping nearby. There was much praying in the shelter those days.

One afternoon, I purposely dallied upstairs to observe one of those bombings from the kitchen stairway's open landing. It had an unobstructed view of the river no more than 300 yards away, where Japanese ships lay docked; that was where the action usually took place. It wasn't long before I saw half a dozen F4U-4 Vought Corsairs gaining altitude in the distant sky before gracefully peeling off, one by one, on their final southerly approach. The planes were drawing a bead on a ship docked in the wharf no more than 300 yards away, almost directly in

27

front of me. As I watched the little spits of flame spewing out of each wing's leading edge, something in the back of my mind warned me that I may have been courting danger, perhaps even taunting death. I remember just standing there, glued to the landing, washed by a strange feeling of terror mixed with the insane joy of daring[4].

The few remaining civilians in the city grew increasingly worried about the constant American bombings and the nightly sky-shine from the escalating guerrillas' nighttime probing of the Japanese defenses in the outskirts of town. Almost to a family, the remaining civilians decided to huddle for safety in Colegio San Agustin, our now-closed boys' school, crowding together to await developments. Our family, of course, followed suit. It didn't take long, however, for the Japanese to catch on to our ruse and force us back to our homes to resume our proper role as hostages in the ever-intensifying American bombings.

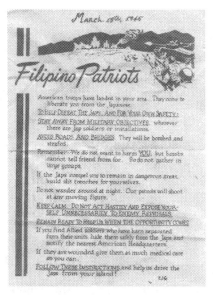

During the last few months of the war, we practically lived by the air-raid shelter, toughing it out through the now almost daily American bombings on nearby Japanese military objectives. One day, a piece of molten anchor from a ship docked on the nearby river came sailing over to our home, crashed through the roof and two floors, and landed almost at our feet. I still remember singeing my fingers when I unwisely reached over to feel the heat of

---

[4] I had many similar adrenaline rushes several years later, running the bulls in Pamplona.

the gnarled, molten object.

Luis and I were sitting on our favorite rooftop observation post on the morning of March 19, 1945, when the sudden roar of a P-38 flying at rooftop level surprised us. Its unexpected appearance took my breath away; I was literally transfixed when I saw the pilot waving at us from behind his canopy as he zoomed past. He was dropping shiny objects which looked like leaflets as he flew past. On retrieving and reading one of the leaflets we learned that the Americans had landed that same day in Molo, a beach a scant ten miles away, where we used to go swimming. The leaflet instructed the civilian population to remain indoors until all was safe. Luis and I jumped up for joy. We had waited more than three years for this event to take place and now, a pilot flying my very favorite warplane, was personally conveying the joyous news to us.

The Japanese stragglers began dynamiting their official buildings and residences in the city that afternoon, setting fire to as many of the remaining houses still left standing. As Dad and I stood behind our house's grilled main door, we observed two Japanese soldiers approaching. One of them toted a Gerry can while the other, a Corporal, demanded to be let in. They were, obviously, intending to set the house on fire.

At that moment, Dad did something startling: standing his ground, he brazenly ordered them to move along. "*Sigue na!*" he bellowed. It was perhaps one of two Filipino phrases he knew; this one meaning: "Move on!" Startled at first by the impertinent command coming from a white, round-eyed civilian, the irate corporal un-slung his rifle and thrust its attached bayonet at Dad, stopping only an inch short of his belly. I was petrified. I couldn't believe Dad's foolhardy display of bravery. But it worked. Thrown aback by Dad's stentorian command, the two soldiers diffidently moved on to the neighboring houses across the street, where, uncontested by absentee owners, proceeded to set them on fire.

The resulting inferno was awesome. The heat from the nearby fires started to set our window canvas awnings on fire. Concerned that the flames would spread and end up consuming our house, Dad ordered the refugees, who had congregated in our house over the preceding hours, to move on to the nearby church of San Jose. There was an unspoken notion that churches made safe havens. As I was about to join the departing group, Dad held me back and asked me to stay behind to help save the house. His request both surprised me and made me inordinately proud. Though I had just turned 14, I felt that I had suddenly crossed some mysterious threshold into manhood.

Dad quickly organized a bucket brigade to haul water up to those already on the roof, dousing it and its eves and awnings in an attempt to cool down the overheating house. Two houses were ablaze across the street, their smoke and flying sparks making it hard to breathe. Our galvanized roof was hot to the touch, while large chunks of concrete from dynamited buildings nearby were crashing down around us.

While dousing the roof, I happened to look down to see a squad of Japanese soldiers marching smartly up Calle Real, apparently headed for the front. It didn't take me long to recognize the unmistakable loping gait and familiar round granny glasses of their leader: Uyeki was in command of the retreating squad! At that moment of sudden recognition, something in me suddenly snapped. Resting my water pail on the roof, I slowly raised my right hand up in the air, curled all fingers down save the middle one, and shot Uyeki one magnificent bird. Furious at the silent insult, he ordered his squad to a halt, pointed at me and ordered them to open fire. I had barely ducked behind a gable when I felt the ominous thud of twelve bullets ripping into the roof around me. In the short span of my brief life, I couldn't remember ever praying with greater fervor.

Someone upstairs must have been listening because, at that very moment, lying face flat on the hot tin roof, I heard the roar of three P-39 Air Cobras swooping down on Uyeki's squad below us, strafing them

30

repeatedly. Inching over to the edge of the roof, I saw the soldiers scattering helter-skelter, taking cover behind several portals along Calle Real. I found it odd how some terrifying moments in life sometimes turn out to be the most exhilarating.

When the fires eventually died down and the crisis subsided, Dad asked me to fetch the family from church. There was great rejoicing when they returned and saw the house still standing. While we slept fitfully that night, we were awakened at midnight by ominous news that Lizarraga's residence, only a couple of blocks from ours, had caught on fire. The wind had kicked up and was blowing the conflagration straight toward our house. The chances of saving it this time were slim.

Dad, once again, ordered us all back to the church, while he remained behind to await developments. It was another of Dad's foolhardy gestures, I thought, but that was Dad. He felt honor bound to save the house entrusted to his care. And with honor at stake, Mom knew no amount of pleading would change his mind. For some strange reason, a Benavente snippet popped into my mind: *"..el honor es patrimonio del alma, y el alma solo es de Dios[5]."*

The church teemed with refugees when we got there, some sleeping fitfully, some coughing, others mumbling prayers above the clicking of rosaries. Outside, an eerie silence hung over the city. I didn't sleep a wink, worrying about Dad. When the first rays of dawn finally shone through the stained glass windows above me, I decide to sneak out of church to check up on him. Quietly slipping out of church, I jumped in and out of the foxholes pocking Plaza Libertad, and slowly crawled my way toward home, all the time fearing the worst. When I finally turned the corner I was greeted by an astonishing sight; the house still stood! The wind had apparently shifted overnight, sparing the

---

[5] Honor is the patrimony of the soul and the soul is only God's

house. Dad stood in front the main gate, arms akimbo, as if daring the world to wrest it away from him.

"What brings you here at this ungodly hour?" he asked, surprised to see me approach. Giving him a big hug, I answered:

"Just checking up on you," I said, trying to sound grown-up.

At that very instant, the pedestal of filial reverence I had built under his feet over a lifetime was transformed into something even more ineffable: a new and deeper father-son bond had blossomed overnight. That overwhelming sensation was to remain with me for years to come. Just then, I felt an even stranger feeling: I *knew* that I had definitely crossed the threshold into manhood.

The events that followed were almost anticlimactic. Dad asked me to go back to church once again and escort the family back home. Their homecoming was even more joyous than the previous one, the night before. There was much hugging and kissing, and weeping for the sheer joy of having survived and being together again.

And then, the shelling started.

The American advance had been temporarily slowed down by landmines set by the Japanese. The Americans were unaware that the Japanese had abandoned town the night before, breaking through the guerrilla noose and headed for the hills for one last stand there. Fearing the recurrence of a brutal house-to-house combat other divisions had encountered in Manila only a month earlier, the 40th Division's commander opted to raze the city with a walk-up shelling tactic before going in. Huddled in the shelter, we heard the shells crumpling ever closer, the thunderous noise growing louder by the minute. The whistling sound of approaching shells was a new and terrifying experience. I'd never heard so many people praying out loud with such unabashed devotion.

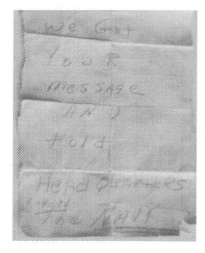

Then, suddenly, miraculously, the shelling stopped. While we were puzzling over the unexpected hiatus, my Basque friend, Iñaki Elordi, turned up with a most bizarre story. The pilot of the artillery-spotting Piper Cub flying over the city had read the sign the Sagrado Corazon nuns had spelled out on the sand in the nearby beach:

"NO JAPS IN CITY"

Suspecting that nuns wouldn't fib, the pilot promptly dropped a monkey wrench with an attached note written on wrapping paper, which read:

"WE GOT YOUR MESSAGE AND TOLD HEADQUARTERS. signed: THE NAVY"

That's all it took for the shelling to stop. The fortuitous event and the nuns' shrewd thinking had saved our lives.

It was almost noon when the first American jeeps rolled down Calle Real with soldiers of a Bomb Disposal Squad. After the land mines were cleared, an endless procession of tanks and troop-laden vehicles followed. The soldiers waved and tossed candy bars, chewing gum and cigarettes to a populace delirious with the joy of liberation. The contrast between these burly warriors and their predecessors was astounding. Much has been written about the frenzy of liberated populations. I can only attest that there are few feelings as poignant as shouting: "Hi, Joe!" to the blond, smiling, youthful doughboys in their olive green uniforms marching down both sides of a street. The salutation is pregnant with the deepest, heartfelt thanks for having been liberated and allowed, literally, to be born again.

Life limped back to normal, but only falteringly. People trickled back from the hills, dazed by the ruin about them. Running water and electricity were restored soon enough, but everything else remained shattered for a long time, almost as if the land's topsoil had been blown away, gone the way of the "Co-Prosperity Sphere," a phrase the Japanese had so boringly touted. Colegio San Agustin took its sweet time reopening. Having had school breaks before, we took the latest one in happy stride.

Those post-war days were like a new chapter in our lives. An empty warehouse near home was occupied by a Special Services outfit whose charter was to provide troops with books, sports equipment, movies, even USO shows. They plied us with such forgotten goodies as baseball gloves and basketballs, books, and delicacies such as Spam and canned butter spread, even GI boots, which I sorely needed. I befriended the outfit's movie projector specialist and got to watch many of the movies I had missed all those war years. My English soon picked up an American twang, something that would stand me in good stead years later.

We met many American Officers during the few months the 40th. Division remained in town. They'd drop in for drinks, evenings, and sometimes even stayed for supper. It was almost like old times. Mom, ever the gracious hostess, managed to breathe one last breath of life into the long-dead *Belle Époque*. Dad humored her and went along with the soirees and candlelit dinners she'd organize.

A young Navy Lieutenant came in from the rain one evening. His bearded smile gave him less the air of a warrior than a poet, which it turned out, he really was. His name was Jac Chambliss, he explained with a Tennessee drawl. His blue eyes twinkled as he explained that his ship had just put into port that morning and that a

34

friend had told him about us. There was a certain grace of motion and unstudied sensitivity about him that belied the inner toughness of an ex-Golden Gloves boxer and a feisty trial lawyer.

Jac struck a resonant chord with Mom when he recognized her hometown's name of Burguete. "Hemingway went fishing near there and wrote about in 'The Sun Also Rises'." Mom, of course, knew.

He offered to send a telegram to my grandmother, in Burguete, to let her know we were alive and well. We later learned that Grandmother had summoned the town doctor to translate the English missive. That was fortunate because she fainted right there, in front of him, from the excitement of learning about our survival. She had given us up for dead, after news of the Manila massacre.

Jac became a regular dinner guest during his ship's stay in port. He'd turn up with a freshly baked loaf of bread which we'd ravenously devour, not having tasted any in years. Mom would serve him Spam, believing it was some gourmet delicacy. She was puzzled when he'd turn it down, asking, instead, for a second helping of Mongo lentil soup. We all found that quite amusing.

He took Luis and me one day on a borrowed Jeep to the big airport on the outskirts of town, to admire a P-61 Black Widow fighter sitting on the tarmac. He explained that its name came from the many Japanese widows this type of airplane caused with its radar's night-fighting capability.

Jac's Liberty ship sailed from Iloilo a few weeks later. Mom kept up a correspondence with him over the ensuing years[6], both of them

---

[6] Almost ten years later, to the day, his oldest daughter, Ann, was in Scotland on her Junior Year abroad program, studying English at St. Andrew's University. Mom, by then a widow and living in Pamplona, invited her to spend Christmas vacations with us. Being home for Christmas myself, we met and fell hopelessly in love. I came to the

being fluent in French and English.

Shortly after the American Army left Panay, a portly, linen-suited Englishman blew into town. He was the Far Eastern representative of the British-owned Hongkong & Shanghai National Bank, sent to reopen his bank's Iloilo branch office. Since all the hotels in town had been leveled, Dad invited Mr. Waite to stay with us.

The gimlet-eyed Mr. Waite was a spitting image of Colonel Blimp. He'd spew out pat little phrases through unmoving lips, in a clipped, self-conscious sort of way. He'd start most sentences with "Actually," and I soon wearied of his puckish hyperbole; things weren't just 'awful'; they had to be "perfectly ghastly," things being either a "sporting jolly good show!" or a "frightful sort of rot, what?"

He came back from his first inspection tour of the bank muttering something about "those dastardly Jap chaps!" for making such a "frightful shambles" of his offices, adding, with upper crusty indignation, "All those checks lying about like a ghastly ticker tape parade!" Luis and I exchanged furtive glances. If he'd only known the wonder and delight of that magnificent battle royal!

He asked for some stationary to write his report one morning after breakfast. Unthinkingly, I provided him with several crisp bond paper sheets. "Absolutely spiffing, what?" said the delighted Englishman, taking the proffered sheets. Suddenly, his eyes focused on the letterhead: there, prominently embossed at the top of the page was the name of his very own Bank! He gawked at the sheets in front of him, pupils distended, jaw dropping in a graceless, jowly gape. To his query "Where on earth did you come by this stationary?" I responded with the serenity of a jack hammer: "Oh, we found them strewn about. Figured

States a year after and married her three years later, during my last year of College.

36

we'd save them for a special occasion. Good thinking, wouldn't you say?" I asked with deadpan expression. "Rawtha!" declared the still perplexed Mr. Waite.

I never figured out whether Mr. Waite's ensuing coolness was to compensate for his having lost it during our little interchange or because of his growing suspicion that he'd been bested by a picaresque young Spaniard. He left town shortly after with a limp upper lip and a definitely drooping pecker.

School eventually reopened, allowing me to finish my interrupted Second Year of High School without any further starts. I remember being forced to write my final exams with my left hand, having broken two metatarsals in my right hand during a bare-knuckled fisticuff incident in school, the week prior to Finals.

The plantations and sugar Centrals that Dad had overseen before the war had been laid low, leaving him without his old responsibilities and a little out of sorts. In compensation for his having saved Elizalde's Iloilo residence, he was offered a new position in the Company's central offices in Manila. The transfer meant that the whole family had to move to the Capital. We made the trip on a Liberty ship, relieving the blisteringly hot passage with frequent salt water showers.

Once named "The Pearl of the Orient," the desolation visited on Manila during the last month of the war was heart-rending. Dad managed to rent a chalet in the Paco district of Manila. Located in one of the city's hardest-fought districts, the house was riddled by a myriad bullet and shrapnel holes, making it resemble more a sieve than a residence. We somehow managed to patch it up enough to stay dry.

I remember attending Mass with Dad at the Augustinian Church in Intramuros on Sundays. The only attendees were the two of us and the celebrant. The church's roof was completely gone, overgrown vines creeping up its outside walls and down almost to the pews inside, birds freely flying around, chirping throughout the celebration. The whole scene felt hauntingly sacred. It became doubly poignant when I learned that the Japanese had herded a sizeable group of Spanish colonials into that very church's crypt one day in February of 1945, during the battle of Manila, and massacred them all by lobbing hand grenades into the jam-packed enclosure. My godfather Goicoechea and all his family perished there that day.

Luis and I were enrolled in the Ateneo de Manila, the city's pre-eminent private High School, within walking distance of home. Our sisters were enrolled in the neighboring nun school of Asunción. Ateneo's original buildings had been razed to the ground. Classes were now held in quaint, Army surplus Quonset huts. My outstanding Jesuit teachers more than made up for the sorry surroundings.

My Junior Year of High School was quite demanding. Fr. Finley, our home room teacher, taught us English and Latin with equal flair. I enjoyed his Creative Writing course immensely, having been hopelessly hooked by the beauty of Jac Chambliss' poetic prose in an essay he left with me, titled "The Psalmist." Fr. Finley also taught us declamation, poetry and, of course, Religion, a subject thoroughly drummed into us with the help of frequent soul-cleansing Jesuit Spiritual Exercises.

Dr. Modry, an elderly Jewish émigré from Austria, taught us advanced Algebra and Trigonometry, subjects made doubly abstruse by the unintelligible English he spoke. I forget the Sociology teacher's name now but I remember impressing both him and my debating opponent on the obscure subject of the American Jury system. Sports were more formal and better organized at the Ateneo than in San Agustin. I thoroughly enjoyed basketball and boxing intramurals, sports in which I excelled, until the afternoon a lightning-fast Filipino boxing contender almost knocked me out cold. I remember having trouble memorizing anything that evening.

Basketball, like boxing, was second nature with Filipinos. Our school's basketball team, the Blue Eagles, was the city's perennial High School champion. The day they played the rival San Beda team in the final championship game that year was unforgettable. The tension between the two schools was such that both bleachers emptied into the court at game's end and got into a glorious free-for-all. I'll never forget seeing our band's bass drummer completely immobilizing an unsuspecting opponent by ramming his instrument down his head.

I remember the parades and endless speeches at the Luneta Park in downtown Manila on July 4th.1946, commemorating the Philippines' independence from the United States. There was great jubilation at the event, some local wry historian jestingly referring to the three historical phases of the country's long road to independence as having lived 400 years in a Spanish convent, 40 years in a Hollywood setting and four years regurgitating Japanese sushi.

Dad had planned to retire just before the war broke out; he had even acquired tickets for the return trip to Spain just before the onset of the war frustrated those plans. The bitter experience and penuries that war had inflicted on his family only augmented his yearning to return to the old sod. His children were approaching a marriageable age and he wanted to make sure they chose Basque partners when the time came. All these considerations only heightened his decision to retire.

When the school year came to an end on March of 1947, he acquired tickets on an American President Liner for the trip back to Spain. We said our goodbyes to Floríng, the young maid who had remained with the family since war began, and left Beltxa, our pet German shepherd, in her care. Fr. Finley and several of my classmates came to the ship to wish us bon voyage. Before I knew it, the ship's horn sounded its deep-throated farewell and we slipped gently out of the wharf and into Manila Bay, past the island of Corregidor and on into the

39

China Sea. I was deeply conscious of the fact that I was leaving the land where I was born, perhaps for good. I was surprised to feel no great qualms at my departure, so strong was my yearning to set foot on the homeland I'd heard about all my life and was about to know firsthand.

Chapter 3

The Homeward Passage

"Patria est, ubicumque est bene[7]"
Marcus Pacuvilus

The President Polk was a slick 15,000- ton vessel boasting a top speed of 18 knots, with a beam broad enough to ensure a relatively stable passage. It had a smallish swimming pool, a spacious lounge, a large dining room, a modest library and, best of all, indoor air-conditioning. There were about a hundred passengers aboard, mostly Americans on a round-the-world cruise. Luis and I got to share a stateroom; my two sisters shared another, while Mom and Dad occupied still another.

I soon made friends with Julian, a 16-year old Canadian passenger, perhaps because Jackie, his cute 14 year-old sister, reminded me of Karmele, my very first flame in Iloilo. We went swimming almost every day and played deck games like shuffleboard and ping-pong. Luis played chess with an elderly Scottish gentleman whose thick brogue made it hard to decipher his frequent "checkmates." Evenings, we'd watch outdoor movies after supper. I remember the very first one, "She Wrote a Book," which I thoroughly enjoyed. Being a voracious reader, I

---

[7] Wherever we are content, that is our country

41

was constantly checking books from the library. I remember reading "The Robe" early in the trip, finding its subject matter similar to that of "Quo Vadis," which I'd read years earlier. They didn't have any Tom Swift books on board.

My siblings and I shared a table at the dining room with one Giovanni Burigotto, a dapple, aged Italian architect who had a definite weakness for food. He shocked Mari Blanca with stories about how he'd been to church only twice in his life, each for the purpose of sidling up to some good looking girl. Mom and Dad shared a contiguous table with Mr. Gabaldón, the stiff-necked Spanish Ambassador to the Philippines, on his way to a vacation to Spain.

I was at first conscious of the elegant attire most passengers wore to dinner. I couldn't help comparing them to our ill-fitting, hand-me-down apparel, hastily acquired in Manila on the eve of our European trip. But I soon got over that uneasiness and settled down to enjoy the ship's amenities. The crew was friendly and the cuisine superb. Our waiter Nick, a Dutchman from Amsterdam, plied us with hearty entrees of roast beef and lobster, always topped with delicious desserts.

I enjoyed repairing to the ship's bow, where I'd lean over the rail for hours on end, feeling the flung spray and the salty sea breeze on my face, watching dolphin and flying fish cavorting near the ship's bow spray. Being out and about all day, I soon acquired a deep tan, which I thought favored me.

We sailed into Singapore five days into the trip. The handsome English villas dotting both sides of the inlet impressed me. We sailed past the large "Empress of Australia" on the way in. Just before docking, small native skiffs sidled up to the ship as it slowed down to a crawl. With their red Muslim fezzes and long, loose robes the noisome natives hawking their wares reminded me of Filipino "*moros*."

We ambled over to the Raffles Hotel when we got ashore next morning. After a haircut and an orange drink at the hotel's restaurant/bar, we went to the Raffles Museum to gawk at the impressive collection of animals and fowl housed there. Malayan workers appeared to move about their business more briskly than their Filipino counterparts. As in the Philippines, most businesses in Singapore were run by Chinese.

A surly taxi driver drove us back to the ship around noon, taking us on an unsolicited grand tour of the town. We drove past large botanical gardens, handsome cricket playgrounds and tall, impressive buildings, some flying the Union Jack. Along the way, I saw my first rickshaw struggling up a hill.

A new batch of mostly Indian passengers came on board that afternoon. Among the new arrivals were four barefoot Buddhist monks attired in bright saffron-colored robes. I was itching to meet them and learn more about their religion, particularly their belief in reincarnation.

From the ship's bulletin board I learned that our next port of call was Penang, a city on the western coast of the Malayan Peninsula. We were excited to see Mr. Waite again. He had been one of the Directors of the Hong Kong Shanghai National Bank who had visited us in Iloilo right after the liberation and now headed the bank's Penang offices.

We spotted land to starboard early next morning. When Penang came into view I figured it to be about the size of Iloilo. The homes around the port area looked neat and well kept. Below us, in the relatively shallow, murky waters, I saw a myriad of red jellyfish bumping against each other. The thought of falling overboard into that carpet of jellyfish made me shudder.

We went on a sightseeing tour as soon as we got ashore. The men driving rickshaws in the wilting heat reminded me a little of Markham's *Man with the Hoe*, with all its "weight-of-centuries-on-their-backs" trimmings. Despite Mr. Gabaldón's reservations about the shore adventure we proposed, he joined Dad, Luis and me on an escapade to a snake temple atop a nearby hill, one of several local places of worship.

The temple's curlicue gables lent it a distinctly Chinese architectural air. Once inside, we found the main hall teeming with small, inch-long vipers sleeping on the bare branches of countless bonsai-like shrubs sitting on squat altars dispersed all around the enclosure. The guide informed us that the reptiles slept during the day, climbing down at night for food; definitely not a place to visit after hours, he added. They stirred to wakefulness when I prodded them but promptly went back to sleep. My temerity displeased Mr. Gabaldón, who refused to follow us into the temple's sanctum sanctorum, where we found a cage with a huge albino python sleeping in it, purportedly the temple's principal deity. I was impressed by its appetite when informed that it was fed several chickens and dozens of eggs every week.

Mr. Waite came aboard that evening to pay his respects to mom and dad, taking them out for a ride around town after supper. His chauffeured limousine was waiting for us early next morning to take us to the private Penang Swimming Club. Its Olympic-sized pool bordered a beach of glistening white sand. I'd never seen a beach with white sand before and was taken by its beauty.

Mr. Waite joined us for Tiffin at the club, preceded by the *de rigueur* cocktails and ginger beer appetizers. I attributed the slightly rancid taste of the butter to the hot weather. Before leaving for work

44

after lunch, Mr. Waite bade us *bon voyage*. Later than afternoon, his limousine drove us back to the ship.

Our next port of call was Colombo, only a few hours away. It was during that leg of the trip that I met Ted Ryberg, the ship's young Radio Officer. Being barely in his twenties, we hit it off from the start. Smitten by wanderlust, he'd taken a year off from College to see the world. He appeared well versed in the classics and dabbled in photography as a hobby. I was amused by some of his anecdotes, particularly the one about once getting lost in Shanghai and almost missing the boat. Detained by Chinese gendarmes when he ended up in an out-of-limits island, he produced the only official-looking document he happened to have on him: his Social Security card. Impressed, the guards let him go.

He and I cornered one of the Buddhist monks after lunch and grilled him about reincarnation. I was amazed to learn that sinners migrated back to Earth after death, reincarnated as dogs or frogs or some other lowly form of life. After several stages of reincarnation, those who'd lived a proper life returned in a more exalted state and finally attained Nirvana. Buddhists, he averred, didn't believe in a Supreme Being. I attempted to enlighten him on the subject with my Jesuit-inspired scholastic arguments for God's existence, all of which seemed to fall on deaf ears. He surprised me with the tidbit about everything, including God, having a beginning. He also believed that God had nothing to do with what transpires on Earth, while, in the same breath, disavowing man's free will. Even to my young ears, his logic sounded a trifle garbled.

Now on a roll, he tried to explain the difference between "real" and "nominal" Buddhists. Most Japanese, he said, were not real Buddhists. I was subsequently intrigued by his enumeration of the Buddhists' five commandments; disapproval of murder, drinking alcoholic beverages, lying, stealing and committing impurities. Not a bad synopsis of the Christian Commandments themselves, I thought.

Buddhists didn't believe in repentance, he pursued. Their religion teaches them not to be sorry; just not to repeat the wrongful act again. They don't believe in war either and are, by definition, conscientious objectors. They don't engage in missionary work, either, which, he explained, resulted in a diminished number of converts and followers.

It was almost dinner time when we finished our little Inquisition. It had been an enlightening discussion, although I didn't think anyone convinced the other. I found the sophistic exercise enlightening, nonetheless.

Later that evening the hulking mountains of Ceylon loomed into view and the lights of Colombo became visible from the stateroom's porthole. The ship's engines slowed down to a crawl that night to ensure a daylight arrival.

We had anchored by the time we woke up next morning. I was surprised to observe the port's lack of a proper wharf, passengers having to board launches to get on and off the ship. Once on shore, we visited several jewelry stores, Ceylon being famous for its rubies and sapphires.

The snake charmers we saw along the way asked exorbitant prices for their display, so we turned them down, hired a dilapidated '37 model Buick taxi and went to visit a Buddhist temple nearby. Posters on its walls suggested discouraging cinnamon root vendors, temple beggars and shoe-shine ragamuffins. Charity donations to the temple were, however, encouraged.

After shedding our shoes at the temple's entrance, we entered the hall and came face to face with three enormous statues of Buddha – one sitting, the other standing, the third reclining. Paintings on the wall depicted the life of Lord Buddha. One of them, the temptation of Buddha, looked suspiciously Christian.

The temple visit was followed by a stop at a zoological park which housed a striking collection of beasts. I was particularly taken by the roar of a resident Bengal tiger as it squirted onlookers with a disgusting spray of urine.

Next morning, Luis Mari, Ted, Paul, the ship's Cadet, and I went for a swim at the Grand Hotel's beach, at the foot of Mt. Lavinia. On our way there, trying to shoo a flock of pigeons that had alighted in front of him as he was crossing an avenue, my brother kicked one of the birds out of the way. A traffic cop who witnessed the incident came rushing toward him, shrilly blowing his whistle.

"You could have kicked my grandmother," he complained bitterly as he got ready to hand my brother a ticket for the grievous misdemeanor. The enormity of the reincarnation lesson recently learned suddenly dawned on me; this cop's granny must have led an unedifying life for having reincarnated into something no better than a lowly pigeon.

After the awkward incident was cleared up, we took a taxi to the Grand Hotel. Shedding our clothes and donning swim suits in the hotel's locker room, we spent a wonderful afternoon at the palm-fringed white sand beach. Stopping at the locker room on the way back, my brother discovered that his brand new leather shoes were missing. Despite lodging a complaint at the manager's office, Luis had to return to the ship barefooted, there to earn an undeserved dressing down from Dad. Later that evening, the Hotel's manager came aboard with Luis' missing shoes, assuring us that he had fired his locker room attendant for dereliction of duty.

After leaving Colombo, we sailed north for the next few days, cruising along the Indian subcontinent's eastern coast. Bombay was our next scheduled port of call. From the vantage point of the promenade deck, I noticed that we were steaming north at a fair clip, with still no land in sight to starboard. I spotted several Chinese junks on the horizon, also heading north. Sea gulls above us cried their baleful, vacant cries, occasionally diving for tidbits of galley-discarded food. Recalling the dove in the Noah story, I surmised that land could not be far away.

That evening, I was surprised to find my brother sitting on a deck chair, unusually bleary eyed. Louis Ludwig, a quaint New York Jew who dabbled in hypnotism, had not quite snapped my brother out of the trance he'd put him under. He subsequently tried to put my friend Julian under a hypnotic spell but the young Canadian fought the attempt, forcing Ludwig to desist. Next day, he tried to hypnotize me in front of a large audience in his stateroom, but was chagrined at his unsuccessful attempt. I later bragged about it to my brother, putting it down to my superior strength of character. He, of course, knew better.

Because half the passengers were getting off in Bombay the next day, a grand Captain's Dinner was organized the night before, complete with American flags, balloons, festoons and noise-makers. I even donned my finest woolen suit for the occasion, only to regret its resulting warmth.

Bombay came into view next morning, its tall buildings visible even from a distance. As we approached, I noticed fewer ocean liners berthed on its docks than in Singapore. Shortly after docking on Alexandra Docks, relatives of the disembarking passengers came aboard to wish them a hearty welcome. Since we didn't have a proper Indian visa, we couldn't go ashore that day.

Natives came on board to carry out their varied chores, some scrubbing the deck, others painting the ship's sides. I was impressed by the Indians' finely chiseled features, their thick beards and Sikh turbans. I also noticed the long, grimy black tunics they wore over baggy pants which drooped down to their bare feet. I found most of them had kind, pleasant faces, while others looked downright sinister. They were a hard working lot and didn't seem to need much supervision.

The morning after we arrived, Ted arranged for the Captain to sign special crew-member permits for Luis and me, so we could go ashore. Assigned officious ranks of 3rd and 4th Radio Officer Assistants, Luis, Ted and Paul and I hopped on a taxi and rode off to the Breach Kandi swimming club. I was shocked by a large sign hanging from the main entrance, which read: "No Indians Allowed." I found it odd that natives anywhere were not allowed to enter an establishment in their own country. I was yet to learn about the concept later labeled "racial discrimination," but found that sign a sobering first whiff of it.

The club's oval-shaped, salt water swimming pool bordering the sea was the largest pool I'd ever been in. We swam in it for endless hours, ate barley bread sandwiches and drank orange crush for lunch. On the way back to the ship, we drove past majestic buildings, the grandest being the Taj Majal Hotel[8], with its impressive 500- room accommodations. The city's avenues were wider than any I'd ever seen before. American car businesses seemed to be flourishing in India, with brands like Ford, Frazer, Packard and De Soto prominently advertised in store windows.

Ted took Luis and me to town that evening to a movie and ice cream sodas. On the way back to the ship, we walked along the avenues' broad sidewalks, literally stepping over sleeping Indians. Ted informed me that municipal workers would gather the dead from among them the

---

[8] Bombed by terrorists almost 66 years later.

49

next morning and take them to a hill nearby for cremation, their ashes later dumped in some sacred river. Adding to the dreadful vignette was the little tidbit about the deceased's navels being the only remains surviving the cremation.

An English priest from a ship anchored next door came to celebrate Sunday Mass next morning in the small chapel set up in our ship's lounge. I served Mass, surprised that I could still remember the Latin responses I'd learned as an acolyte in Iloilo, years earlier. I found out that there were about 5 million Catholics in India and thought that St. Francis Xavier must have been a busy missionary during his Goa stopover, centuries earlier.

Because of the simmering friction between Indians and whites, someone commented that it wouldn't have been safe to go ashore a month earlier. I had detected a certain impudence in the natives' attitude towards us. Some street posters still read: "We don't need the white monkeys. Let them go home!" Feelings for self-rule were running high. It was, after all, only three months before India won her Independence from Britain and the natives were restless. One could sense the winds of revolution definitely brewing. Some attributed the natives' unrest to envy of the independence the Filipinos' had only recently acquired from the Americans. Freedom is, after all, a catching sort of thing, hard to ignore or long suppress.

From the ship's rail that afternoon, we watched a snake charmer on the wharf, hawking his wares. For two Rupees, he offered to demonstrate a lethal combat between a cobra and a mongoose, two known natural enemies. After collecting the fee from the onlookers, he pulled a mongoose and a cobra from their respective cages and set them loose on the ground. The two creatures eyed each other warily at first. The cobra then struck several times at the mongoose, which neatly evaded the thrusts and waited for the cobra to grow sluggish enough before striking back. Avoiding the cobra's fourth lunge, the mongoose quickly turned its head, grabbed the snake's head in its jaws, crushed it and put an end to the nature show.

Thirty new passengers came on board that afternoon. Not allowed to bring her two pet dogs aboard, a French lady stormed back down the gangplank in a huff, shouting imprecations at the restraining Officer. In the midst of this commotion, two regally attired Indian princesses stood on the quay waving goodbye to someone who had just come on board.

There was a less festive mood that evening at the dining room than the night we sailed into Bombay, four days earlier. Mari Blanca's piano playing lightened up the mood somewhat at suppertime.

We noticed a pleasant change in temperature as we sailed out of Bombay, turning unseasonably cool during the next several days, as we approached the Red Sea. We had to pile on extra blankets at night and the swimming pool was closed for the duration. The unexpected calmness of the Indian Ocean inspired me to write a poem on the subject, entitled "The Great Defiance," which, if memory serves, started:

"Avast, ye Indian waters cease to cry
Who is it that on my flesh cuts deep?"

I thought the poem banal but Ted seemed to like it and pinned it up on the ship's bulletin board. A British lady who happened to read it that afternoon enthused about it and pronounced it 'practically wonderful'. I remained unconvinced.

It wasn't long before we sailed past Aden, then a British refueling station on the southern tip of the Arabian Peninsula. We still hadn't seen the coast of Africa but the maritime traffic seemed to grow busier as we approached the Red Sea. As usual, dolphins performed their graceful acrobatics, attempting to keep up with the ship.

When we finally dropped anchor in the bay of Suez I sensed that we were on the eve of discovering a new world. At last we saw land on both sides of the ship, and that was reassuring. The deck Steward pointed out the spot where the Israelites were purported to have crossed the Red Sea when they abandoned Egypt. I was surprised to discover that the Red Sea was not red at all. It got its name, someone explained, because of the reddish sunset glow the coastal Arabian mountains cast on it. A less romantic, but probably more scientific theory attributed the color to some kind of red algae tingeing that particular sea.

Several Government officials, a medical doctor and a pilot came on board when we dropped anchor in Suez Bay. All of them looked swarthy, like Indians, and wore heavy woolen clothes. A few passengers got off the ship on an excursion to Cairo and the pyramids. We'd pick them up in Alexandria two days later.

We started up the Suez Canal that afternoon at a much reduced speed, the canal being only twice the ship's width. Its construction was said to have cost $15 million, a respectable sum those days. A large monument at the Canal's entrance commemorated the spot where Mary and Joseph were supposed to have crossed into Egypt almost two millennia earlier. I thought all these biblical migrations of Jews to and from Egypt rather odd, considering how little they cared for each other. Life must have been harsh in the Holy Land.

It turned noticeably chillier as we proceeded up the 80-mile waterway to Port Said. The Egyptian side of the canal was lush, with handsome homes and luxuriant greenery, while only barren desert was visible on the Sinai Peninsula. About a third of the way up the canal, we sailed onto a large lake. Buoys separated the two-way lake traffic, with shipwrecks and remnants of vessels bombed by the Germans during WWII visible on the distant shores of the lake. We also saw a monument dedicated to the defenders of the Canal during the First World War. I thought it was remarkable to see mementos of two different world wars in the same spot.

After a change of pilots at the halfway point, we proceeded up the canal, having been given priority due to our ship's passenger and mail-carrying status. Once again, lovely scenery appeared on the Egyptian banks as we proceeded up the canal. A highway lined with fir trees wound its way along the western bank of the canal, car traffic stopping to wave at us as we sailed past. A fierce sandstorm kicked up shortly after, forcing us to seek shelter inside the ship.

The stop at Port Said next morning was utterly forgettable. We found the local population surly and unpleasant and were glad to get back on the ship and proceed to Alexandria. We sailed past the De Lesseps statue on the way out and entered the choppy Mediterranean waters.

We arrived in Alexandria next morning. Having heard of their once-famous library being accidentally burned by the Romans, I was eager to visit its ruins. I went ashore with three British passengers and spent the morning touring the town in style. Commenting on the numerous Roman statues we drove past, our taxi driver apprized us of how much Egyptians' disliked Italians, remembering how their city had been bombed by them in 1942.

I don't recall visiting the ruins of the Alexandrian Library but we stopped at some Roman ruins with ancient underground altars and baths. We saw catacombs with embalming rooms and entombed mummies. The tour's highlight, however, was Cleopatra's needle, an imposing 88-ft tall column, built from four solid pieces of granite. We stopped at the city's Botanical gardens, once some ruler's private gardens. After the requisite visit to the local zoo, we stopped at the Cecile Hotel. After lunch there, we stopped at a jewelry store where I was struck by the beauty of a young Egyptian salesperson. I was utterly captivated by the lightness of her skin, her grey green eyes and her exotic fragrance. She was the first truly attractive woman I'd ever seen. I was reminded of how another Egyptian woman had captivated no less than two Caesars.

Back on the ship by mid afternoon, we met the group of passengers who had gone ashore at Port Said to visit Cairo, the pyramids and the Pharaohs' tombs. Their tales made me a little envious. The seas were choppy when we sailed out of Alexandria into the Mediterranean. Most passengers got properly sea-sick and the dining room was almost empty that evening.

The fire drill next day was one of the few distractions of the day, the other being sighting the island of Crete from afar and seeing snow for the first time in my life on its mountain tops. We were scheduled to cross Messina Strait the following afternoon and were promised the grand show of an erupting Mt. Etna. Later that day, Ted taught me an ingenious way of telling north using only one's wristwatch. If on the northern hemisphere, pointing the watch's hour hand toward the sun and bisecting the angle between it and the minute hand determined north, or some such.

Temperatures dropped to 40° F the next day. For the first time in my life, I felt the strange sensation of fingers numbed by cold. The Bishop's wife and several Chinese ladies competed for the fanciest fur coats on board that day. I was reminded of peacocks showing off their colored tails in their stamping ground.

The southern coast of Italy came into view that afternoon. Lovely villages with green meadows and dry river beds were discernible in the lowlands, while snow capped the high peaks. It was March and spring must have already sprung. This was Europe, I thought, with its mysterious changes of seasons. It made me feel as if we were almost home. The Italian passengers on board were perfectly jubilant on sighting their land, at long last.

We sailed past the Strait of Messina that afternoon, with the City of Messina on one side and Riga on the other. We were told we'd witness an erupting Mt. Stromboli that evening, but it turned out to be a false alarm.

I woke up the next morning to see Mt. Vesuvius through the porthole, majestic despite the slight cloud cover. Unlike the perfect cone of Mt. Mayón in Luzon, Vesuvius appeared disfigured by a small hump on its side. Naples, a magnificent city, lay at the foot of the mountain. As we sailed into the bay, we saw an imposing castle sitting atop a small hill in front of us. The city itself appeared scarred by bomb craters and other war wreckage. Two British Destroyer Escorts were anchored near the docks, alongside rusty Italian U-Boats and several sunken Italian warships.

Italian port authorities came aboard the moment we docked. I half expected them to act frostily with Allied passengers, considering the damage inflicted upon their city during the war. I was wrong; American GI's had apparently been their usual generous selves with the liberated population. Italians seemed to favor Americans over the British, believing the latter to be too stiff-necked and self-conscious.

The port authorities stamped our Spanish passports promptly but appeared less hurried when it came to granting visas to American and British passengers. It was, I suspected, a case of tit-for-tat, probably aware that the Italian passengers on board had not been allowed to go ashore to visit Bombay, Suez, Port Said or Alexandria. British insensitivity toward Italians may have been due to Italy's having been an Axis contender. Old wounds heal slowly.

I was surprised to see nothing but Caucasians around me when I came ashore. To my amazement, even street sweepers were light skinned. Everybody's heavy winter coats also surprised me. But I couldn't help noticing a small group of barefoot, sunken-eyed ragamuffins holding out their beggars' cups, begging for alms. But what impressed me even more were nuns and priests discretely begging for alms from the passengers. My heart went out to them.

The attire of the port authority personnel and local carabinieri reminded me of fascist officers in the Fox Movie Tone shorts I saw before the war, and suspected they might be wearing left-over uniforms from the Mussolini era. I also noticed that most commercial transactions between the locals and the passengers were conducted using American cigarettes as barter currency. Black market operations were conducted in broad daylight, authorities looking the other way. American currency in the black market fetched twice as many Lira as in the official exchange.

A dilapidated taxi took us on a sightseeing tour after breakfast. Store windows displaying all imaginable goods made an impression on me. People strolling along cobblestone streets appeared well heeled and prosperous. Our first stop was at a coral and cameo factory outside town, where we lingered a while to admire their workmanship. Despite the heavy downpour outside, we decided to proceed on our planned visit to Pompeii.

Our first stop there was the large amphitheater, complete with baths and gladiators' living quarters. I gawked at the town's ancient ruins, starting with the lead-lined gutters along its sinuous streets, marble sign posts, fountains in home patios, temples with sacrificial tables, and a large forum strewn with a myriad of pillar stumps. My attention was quickly caught by two human cadavers inside a glass showcase, their bones showing through cracked plaster casts.

Our guide took us through some ancient houses of ill repute where, in wide-eyed wonderment, I observed the titillating mosaics and captivating frescoes of naked women of old Pompeii. It was perhaps this tour de force that made my sister Mari Blanca feel suddenly indisposed, forcing us to cut our Pompeian visit short. On the way back to the ship, we stopped at a wayside inn and ate the most delicious spaghetti I'd ever tasted.

Our driver waxed eloquent when informing us that all Italians admired Mussolini and considered him a great ruler. Things ran smoothly then, when he was in control, the taxi driver averred. He built

56

hospitals, schools, roads and countless housing projects for the people. The taxi driver's adulation reminded me that a plebe's approval of politicians depended upon what it could pry from them, *gratis et amore.* In other words, they hankered for *panem et circencem.*

Our ship was expected to leave the next morning for an unscheduled stop in Livorno, a port halfway between Naples and Genoa. The extra stopover implied that we'd arrive at Genoa one day too late to make our connection to Barcelona on the Spanish ship on which we had made reservations. Dad had to make arrangements to disembark in Livorno and make an overland trip to Genoa that night, by either train or bus.

As we sailed toward Livorno, I noticed that the ship's engines had suddenly stopped and that the ship had changed direction; we were now heading south instead of north. Ted explained that the ship's sudden course-reversal was meant to avoid a rogue mine field reportedly floating in our path. After a few zigzag maneuvers, we resumed our northward journey and arrived at Livorno in mid afternoon. As in Naples, the port was littered with war debris. Skirting the obstacles, we docked alongside a makeshift wharf, which consisted of a sunken ship's deck sans its superstructure. The city beyond appeared in utter ruins, an unpromising omen for beginning a land voyage.

After bidding our farewells to shipmates and acquaintances, I came down the gangplank for the last time, already feeling homesick for the President Polk. She had taken us on an unforgettable 38-day journey, halfway around the world.

Once ashore, we discovered that there were no trains or buses out of Livorno for Genoa. For an outrageous price, two disreputable-looking drivers were willing to drive us the 450 km overland route to Genoa on two separate conveyances, one an antediluvian taxi, the other an improbable motor tricycle. I was assigned to escort the luggage-loaded tricycle, while the rest of the family piled up on the taxi.

No sooner had our small convoy struck out of Livorno than Giovanni, my driver, lost contact with the others. There were no cell phones then so communicating with them was not possible. I found myself utterly stranded, literally in the middle of nowhere. More disturbing yet, Giovanni decided to switch conveyances, claiming that the original tricycle was malfunctioning. Standing in the cold drizzle, I watched him and two other men transfer the luggage from one tricycle to the other, helplessly wondering whether he was really having mechanical trouble, as I gathered from my poor Italian, or whether he was merely trying to bump me off and abscond with the luggage, covering his tracks with the switcheroo. It was an unsettling thought.

Things proceeded from bad to worse as we started struggling up the Apennines. With typically-expansive Italian gestures, Giovanni informed me that he was a card-carrying member of the Communist party. I could scarcely believe my ears. Not having ever come across any such political incubus before, I now found myself sitting next to one. With my faltering Italian, I could hardly expect to dissuade him of his political persuasion. Giovanni merely grinned at my obvious discomfort. My attempts at proselytizing Buddhist monks, English colonialists and Italian communists during that short span of time were enough to make me chuckle under my breath. I couldn't help musing on how youth, in its pie-eyed innocence, feels it has the right to challenge customs, traditions and institutions that run counter to his own strongly-held beliefs. I found solace in someone's reflection that youth was, after all, something old folks would love to have but that only the young possessed.

What happened next really set me quaking: reaching over, Giovanni pulled a hand gun from the glove compartment in front of me. After briefly checking if it were loaded, he replaced the firearm back in the compartment and announced, ominously:

"*Molto banditi in questa montagna!*"

"That's great!" I thought to myself. "Now I know even *he* is worried!" Giovanni tried to reassure me, explaining in slow, measured, but not-altogether intelligible Italian, that only armed military convoys dared cross these mountains those early post-war days.

"But not to worry," he added comfortingly. "The *banditi* don't come out when it's foggy, like this. They can't see."

Dubious consolation, I thought to myself, noticing that neither could we. The fog was now rolling down the mountainside like veritable wads of cotton. My side of the tricycle had no windshield wipers, which only made matters worse. When visibility turned truly opaque, Giovanni asked me to get out of the tricycle and walk in front of his headlights to avoid going over the precipice. I was terrified. The little open penknife inside my overcoat pocket offered little comfort. Here I was, barely sixteen, in a strange land, hardly able to see even the road under my feet, walking in front of a communist with a loaded handgun! When the fog lifted briefly and I came back to my seat, I started humming songs to myself to try keeping awake. Just before nightfall, we drove past the city of Pisa and saw its leaning tower. I guessed it was leaning about 25° from vertical and wondered how long it'd survive fighting gravity that way.

The Apennine nightmare abated somewhat when we drove up to a mountain inn and stopped for petit choux and coffee. Ever since then, Italian coffee has reminded me of that dense, dark potion, with dregs so thick they could make one's chest sprout hair forthwith, while keeping one awake for the rest of his life.

We stopped several times along the way to straighten out the two rolled-up Chinese carpets that threatened to roll off the top of the luggage rack. Already in the environs of Genoa, we stopped for coffee in Spezzia, a once picturesque town, now displaying the ravages of war.

Despite all my misgivings, Giovanni eventually deposited me and the luggage in the agreed-upon meeting place in Piazza di Ferrari[9], not far from the port of Genoa. It was two o'clock in the morning and I was greatly relieved to join the rest of the family there, having long since given them up for lost. They, too, were deliriously happy to see me.

After an hour's shut-eye, we ate an extended breakfast at a local Ristorante before heading for the wharf in search of the Spanish ship that was to take us on to Barcelona. There was a bit of a fuss at the port authority offices because our passports had not been properly stamped in Livorno. By 10 o'clock that morning we were installed in our staterooms in the Ciudad de Valencia, a smallish 2000 ton vessel due to leave two hours hence. I found the accommodations a far cry from the Polk's but it was only a short haul to Barcelona, and they would have to do. An added inconvenience was that our staterooms lacked proper bathrooms, having to share a toilet with other passengers.

There were about 20 passengers in the First Class dining room that evening and the service was passable. Much to Dad's delight, the Spanish food served aboard was tasty and reminded him of home, but I found their brown, wild oat bread a sorry substitute for the American wheat brand I was used to. All the women got sea sick as soon as we sailed into the rough waters of the Golfo de León. There were only five passengers for supper that evening at the dining room.

---

[9] Working in the Naviera Aznar Shipping Company in Bilbao three years later, I corresponded with our Genoa Agents, Fratelli Ciccero, with offices in that same Piazza.

The seas were still rough next morning. Only the three Lacambra men came down to breakfast, which consisted of coffee, buttered buns and apple jelly. Little did I know that that would be our frugal Continental breakfast fare from here on.

Chapter 4

Pamplona

"..Yours is the Earth and everything that's in it,
And - which is more – you'll be a Man, my son!"

If
Rudyard Kipling

We were scheduled to dock in Barcelona by ten that evening. I saw the coast of Spain for the first time that afternoon. The sight of my mother country gave me a warm feeling inside. I thought the picturesque little villages along the Costa Brava were beautiful. The weather turned chilly outside and I had to put on my wool overcoat to ward off the unfamiliar cold. Chatting with a fellow passenger that evening, I learned that there were, indeed, bandits in the Apennines those days. I concluded that the rolling fog that enveloped us in the mountains that evening had been a blessing, after all.

It was eleven o'clock that evening when I first sighted the lights of Barcelona, then a city of a little over a million people. Its sprawl impressed me, as did the endless traffic headlights visible on its coastal roadways. I felt shivers of pride when I saw the Plus Ultra monument at the port's entrance, commemorating Columbus' discovery of a new and far-away land. After sailing past a fort-like structure, we finally docked in one of the piers.

At first we didn't recognize any family members among the throng of people waiting at the dock. Moments later, however, Mom spotted her elder sister, Seve, in the crowd, standing by Dad's sister, Ramona. They had just got off a taxicab and were waving excitedly at us. When they finally came on board they barely recognized each other, not having seen one another in 19 years. They hugged and kissed interminably, Mom commenting that her sister's voice had changed. I was struck by Tia Seve's fine features and deep blue eyes, which reminded me a little of my brother's. Tia Ramona, the shorter of the two, had warm, expressive eyes which made her instantly likeable. They couldn't wait to show us off to the rest of the family in Navarre, they said.

We went ashore after having our passports checked and drove to a fancy hotel overlooking the broad Avenue of Las Ramblas. I spent my first night in Spain, pleasantly surprised by the absence of mosquito nets. Next morning, after a frugal Continental breakfast, our aunts took us on a tour to see the highlights of town. We first visited Gaudi's Sagrado Corazón church, a cathedral still in progress today. We then visited the impressive Montjuich Monastery on the heights of Tibidabo, overlooking the city. Next stop was the El Pueblo Español, a lovely mini replica of towns representative of the different regions of Spain. It was, I could tell, a beautiful country.

The stylishly dressed, stiletto-heeled, heavily made-up women and their elegantly suited, well shod escorts walking the broad Barcelona avenues clashed with our aunts' dire accounts of an impoverished, downtrodden Spain. They were, I suspected, simply trying to prepare us for the rough road ahead. From everything I heard, postwar Spain promised to be a sobering experience.

I didn't take long for my first roseate impressions of the country to turn drossy. Food was severely rationed and gasoline was a scarce commodity. Except for tramways and the few, odd looking coal gas-burning (*gasógeno*) taxis, people traveled mostly on foot, which made me wonder about the high heels women wore.

It wasn't long before I started sensing a general malaise among the population. That was not altogether surprising considering that the country had just suffered a recent Civil War with a million dead. That grimness was compounded by the unwarranted ostracism accorded Spain by the international community for having briefly flirted with the Axis during WW II[10]. Spain had been blackballed by the United Nations and temporarily deprived of membership in that august body.

Tia Seve's primary concern was to have us properly clothed. I believe both of my aunts were slightly shocked by our appearance, openly admitting that we reminded them of war refugees, which, in a sense, we were. I had been mortified by that feeling all along.

After outfitting us properly, we took the train to Pamplona, where Tia Ramona's family lived. Tio Enrique, her husband, was a jovial, slightly balding, inconsequential little man who owned and ran a hardware store on Calle Mayor. The plan was to move in with their family in their Calle Mayor flat until adequate lodgings could be found elsewhere. We shared the living quarters with their family on the floor above the store, but though the living quarters were adequate, the living arrangement felt a little tight.

Shortly after arriving in Pamplona, we met dad's other sister, Tía María, as well as our numerous cousins. Since most of them were in their teens, we got along famously with them all. From the day we arrived, cousin Santi, who was a year older than I, took me under his wing and introduced me to many of his classmates in the local Marist

---

[10] Germany and Italy had supplied Franco war materiel during the Civil War. As payback, Franco later allowed two Spanish volunteer Divisions to fight the Russians in Stalingrad. His subsequent refusal to allow passage of Hitler's armies through Spain to reinforce Rommel in North Africa, was considered an inconsequential gesture.

school he attended.

It didn't take long to get used to the daily evening routine of the *paseo*, the stroll up and down Paseo Sarasate and the Taconera Gardens. More than just exercise, the strolls provided the opportunity of walking past pretty girls and greeting them with pining "*hola's*". Santi's classmates took it onto themselves to verse me on the finer points of the Navarran vernacular, complete with salty jokes and nuanced gutter lore, all of which soon got me and Santi in trouble at the dinner table.

Tia Ramona's cooking more than made up for the closeness of the Calle Mayor quarters. I still remember her exquisite *Ajoarriero, Arroz a la Valenciana* and *Piquillo* pepper omelets. The sweetness of Spanish fruit was one of my many pleasant surprises. Weekends, Santi, my brother and I would ride our bikes on excursions to the countryside. Riding by the first vineyards we came across, we'd stop and lie under someone's grapevine and stuff ourselves sick on the dark, luscious grapes. On approaching the town of Puente la Reina, we'd clamber up some farmer's cherry trees to gorge ourselves silly on the forbidden fruit. After a few such unsanctioned incursions, the orchard's owner finally caught on. Surprising us one afternoon stealing his cherries, he peppered our rear ends with salt shot. The resulting itch and bruises took a while to heal.

Residents of Calle Mayor bragged about its being one of the oldest streets in our neck of the medieval city. Everybody knew everybody else and greeted each other every morning with great bonhomie. There were no less than three large churches along the ancient street, all built during the dark ages. The Pamplona of the '40s was still a very devout city, boasting its own seminary with no fewer than 500 young aspirants to the clergy. An old tradition in Navarra called for at least one member of the family to take up the cloth. Two of my first cousins had already joined the Jesuits and the Capuchins, and it was all that I could do to dampen my aunts' ardors, suggesting that I, too, join the religious ranks. I assured them that marriage had always been a priority in my life, a shrewd argument that curbed their zeal momentarily.

I still remember the dank, stuffy atmosphere inside the somber church of San Cernin, near home. I was intrigued to learn that the wobbly wooden planks along the floor of its central nave were actually lids of individual tombs of long-dead devotees. I remember having to kneel in front of the priest every time I went to Confession there, always feeling queasy about his cradling my face in his hands during the absolution, a practice no doubt meant to lend emphasis to the ritual. Those confessions were soul-rending. It was on such occasions that I longed for the old Irish priest in Iloilo with whom we'd confess in Spanish, knowing full well he not only didn't understand the language but was stone deaf, to boot.

Calle Mayor was a quaint medieval sort of main street. Gypsy knife sharpeners turned up occasionally, advertising their services with shrill, distinctive pan-flute whistles. Every morning, like clockwork, a milkman came around with his donkey-drawn cart, loaded with large cans of milk which he bodily distributed to housewives on the different floors. Busy delivering his milk one day, my cousin Pocha and I grabbed a can of turpentine and a brush from his father's hardware store, dashed out to the dozing donkey and dabbed its rear end with the stinging substance. The results were electric. The donkey and its cart took off like greased lightning, launching milk cans as it went. The upheaval somehow reminded me of the carabao incident in Igbarás, years earlier.

After a few days' stay in Pamplona, Mom decided it was time to visit her family in the Pyrenees. We all piled up on the *La Montañesa* bus one afternoon and wove our way up the steep mountain road to Burguete, a pretty little town with no more than a few hundred inhabitants, fast by the Pyrenean foothills. Clear mountain water purled down channels cut along each side of its *Calle Unica*. Lining the street were ancient, neatly whitewashed Basque houses, each with a riot of geraniums gracing its window planters.

67

I thought the family's small Hotel Loizu was the prettiest of the lot. It had been built in the early 19th century by my great grandfather Loizu to serve as a wayside inn for coal and wood merchants, now grown into a reputable 2-star hotel, renowned mostly for its excellent fare. It was efficiently managed by my grandmother Amachi, her daughter Tia Seve and her granddaughter, Maribel.

Grandmother Amachi and Tia Seve's family were waiting for us with bated breath when we came off the bus. Tears rolled down the old lady's cheeks as she embraced her long-lost daughter, whom she hadn't seen in 19 years. Mom was equally moved. In a tumble of words and among the many subjects they touched upon was the telegram Jac Chambliss had sent Amachi via the Red Cross, right after our liberation, informing her that we'd survived the Japanese atrocities in the Philippines. The town Doctor, who had originally been summoned to translate the English telegram, was still around and was called in to help retell the story. That whole episode was as touching as a Greek drama. This time around, though, Amachi didn't pass out because she'd heard the good news before.

I soon noticed that the men in the household blustered a lot but seemed to serve no other function than that of mere onlookers in the overall scheme of things. My first cousin Alberto was almost exactly my age, and we hit it off from the start. Tio Luis, his dad, made him work like a serf, making him get up at some ungodly hour every morning to milk the cows, clean the stables and check up on the family's mares and sheep grazing in the upland meadows, all before breakfast. Alberto grew up untutored and untamed, neglected and unloved by a gruff father who left him no role model to go by. His basic schooling consisted in briefly attending an elementary school in France, supposedly more for discipline than for education. It didn't take him long to abscond from the hostile atmosphere and sneak back home through the mountain passes he knew so well

One fine March morning, Alberto took Luis and me to visit the ancient monastery of Roncesvalles, only a mile north of Burguete. Our first stop there was the monastery's cloister, still with remnants of the previous winter's snows. It may have been old, crusty corn-snow but it was good enough for a first exhilarating brotherly snowball fight. Alberto then showed us around the Monastery's small museum. It held memorabilia of the famous battle fought in that same corner of the world in 778 AD, when the Basques trounced Roland, one of Charlemagne's peers commanding his king's retreating rearguard army.

I quite enjoyed my first and subsequent visits to the family's Hotel Loizu in Burguete. I still remember the abominable, yellow *Ideales* cigarettes Alberto and I smoked in the woodshed, away from his father's watchful eye. Unlike Pamplona, food at the Loizu was always un-rationed, fresh and plentiful. I had a particular weakness for their farm eggs and *longaniza* sausage for breakfast and, in the early summertime, the thick cream desserts piled high with sweet, wild strawberries that literally melted in one's mouth. And how forget the town fiestas of San Juan in late June. It was there that I danced my first dance ever with a girl, my first cousin, Maribel. As soon as it turned dark on that midsummer night's fiesta, they'd light bonfires and jump over the embers, a ritual harking back to a pre-Christian era.

Pamplona, too, had its own charms, especially during the early July festival of *San Fermín*. I ran the bulls at the *encierro* for the first time that year. All my cousins and friends ran the bulls and it was a foregone conclusion that I would too. It gave me an unbelievable adrenaline rush, seeing those big black beasts bearing down on me before I could barely dive out of their way, praying that they'd pass me by and keep on going. While reveling at the bullring with the Oberena gang that first San Fermin afternoon, I happened to sit behind someone who had run that morning and still bore a perfect bull's hoof print neatly imprinted in the back of his white shirt. Judging from his rowdy behavior, he was probably too inebriated to feel the full brunt of the bull's half-ton weight on him.

Running the bulls was a gutsy and dangerous affair, bearable only because of peer pressure. I'll never forget how, on a later *San Fermín* run, a charging bull neatly straddled my left leg between its two horns and gently wafted me up in the air, tossing me clear over a street barrier. I was fortunate enough to land on an unsuspecting spectator, who, luckily, softened my fall, making me suffer no more damage than a bruised ego.

Manolete, the foremost matador of the day, fought in one of the first bullfights I ever witnessed. I was stunned by the man's mastery of his *muleta,* pulling one *natural* pass after another with such dexterity that he managed to turn and steer that bull back and forth for a dozen passes without himself having to move his feet beyond a space wider than a floor tile. After artfully dispatching the bull, he was awarded the bull's tail and both ears, trophies typically granted for any masterful performance[11].

---

[11] Tragically, Manolete was gored to death a month later in the Andalucian town of Linares, while trying to outshine Dominguín, a then-leading competitor.

Tio Enrique's hardware store was a great gathering place. While lending him a hand selling screw drivers and chicken wire to his clientele, I had a chance to meet some interesting visitors who'd drop in just to chat. Fr. Larequi, the cemetery's chaplain, was one of these frequent visitors. He always had some improbable story to tell about "Larequi's garden," as most people called his cemetery. The one that impressed me most was how, the night before someone's burial, he'd rig up an alarm system inside the deceased's casket to ensure that his, or her death hadn't been misdiagnosed, and came alive during the night. We've all probably had nightmares like that in our lifetimes.

Tio Francisco Urreaga, husband of dad's aunt Claudia, was another frequent visitor. He wore an eye patch over an eye lost to an irate buggy driver's horsewhip in an argument in the Philippines, years earlier. Tio Francisco, now retired, had worked in the Philippines for the Navarran firm of Ynchausti & Co. and had convinced my dad to come work with him in the islands. In his visits to Calle Mayor he was fond of recounting the story about an American entrepreneur who owned a tramway system in Iloilo. In pidgin Spanish, the American would admonish his ticket collector for ordering the conductor to get the tramway under way. *"Tú no puede dise 'váminos'"* he'd grumble. *"Solo me puede dise 'váminos!'"* Funny how silly stories like that will stick with you.

Dad rented a large house in Ituren that first summer. It was a quaint little town near his hometown of Elizondo, in the Pyrenean hinterlands. Our neighbors, the Iturbes, recent émigrés from Argentina, had a daughter, Merche, who turned me on enough to make me hop on my one-speed bike every weekend and ride the 40 kilometers from Pamplona to Ituren. Halfway there, the 16-km. climb up Mt.Velate was so steep and demanding that I'd have to hang on to the rear of any truck that happened to be wheezing up the mountain at that moment. On reaching the crest, I'd let go and race it downhill, on the other side of the mountain. In one such daredevil occasion, while speeding downhill

71

trying to beat the rolling fog, I almost ran into a kilometer post masked by the fog. Mulling over the near miss, I brushed it off as something that would have been for a worthy cause. After all, the old saying went: *Amor vincit omnia.*

Late that summer, my sister Mari Blanca decided to become a nun. She had had a religious vocation ever since her days in Iloilo's Sagrado Corazon High School. The Sisters of Charity there must have impressed her enough for her to want to join their Order. Unconvinced that her decision was the right one, Dad at first tried to dissuade her. My sister's determination, however, carried the day. She left home to join the Sisters of Charity as a postulant, her first assignment being that of nurse duty in the local Military Hospital.

Winters were cold in Pamplona. I remember seeing the first real snowfall just before Christmas that first year. I thought seeing one's breath in the cold air was fun but hated the itchy woolen long johns I'd have to wear to ward off the cold. Burguete, of course, was different. There were always fun things to do there in the winter.

The first frost always signaled the *cherriboda*[12] in Burguete, the yearly slaughtering of the pig. The men of the house dispatched one of the huge pigs that had been fed leftovers during the preceding year. Eager to participate in the slaughter, Tío Luis, jestingly assigned me the job of grabbing onto the pigs tail and pulling it with all my might during the slaughter. Naively believing it was an important part of the ritual, my determined pulling brought on laughs and merriment all around.

Once the beast had been dispatched, boiled, shaved and quartered, the town's womenfolk who had congregated in the large hotel kitchen prepared the hams and *chorizos*, the pig's feet, snout and, of

---

[12] Pig wedding

course, the *callos,* its entrail delicacies. All this effort culminated in a great family supper that evening. Some mysterious pig's gland called *shahmes* was reserved for the master of the house's enjoyment.

Alberto taught me how to ski after the first snows in Burguete that year. I watched him fashion his own primitive skis out of two carefully leveled pine boards with leading edges properly bent upward. After rigging spring-loaded boot straps midway up the skis, he finished his chef d'oeuvre by applying several coats of wax on the skis' undersides, with the help of a hot iron.

Early next morning, he took me to a small promontory overlooking the frozen Urrobi brook, behind the hotel. I would have to ski down the short incline for starters, he said. Asked how I'd brake before running into the barbed wire fence posted only inches beyond the frozen brook, he suggested coming to a full stop by sitting down hard on the snow just before running into the fence. What he didn't explain was that where I was supposed to apply this braking maneuver was over a very thin coat of iced-over Urrobi. His raucous laughter seeing my bottom sink into the shallow brook told the whole story of how I'd been taken, once again.

My High School diploma had no standing in Spain. To prepare me for the last Baccalaureate year and satisfy that requirement, Dad enrolled me in a local Academy specializing in Higher Math, Physics and several other technical subjects. The Headmaster, a serious yet friendly scholar, took me under his wing. I found the subjects easy and pleasurable and discovered short cuts and easier approaches to them than I'd learned up to that point.

The Academy had several eclectic students, one of whom I soon befriended. He enjoyed telling stories about his odyssey in Russia as a volunteer in one of the Blue Divisions sent to Stalingrad to fight the Russians. He explained how they almost froze to death in the Russian front, dressed as they were in summer uniforms. Mercifully, they were captured by the Russians and sent to a concentration camp. He was always amused by the stark difference between the pliant, fun-loving, opera-singing Italian prisoners and the ornery, unruly Spaniards. The latter became such personae non grata with the Camp Commandant that they were soon shipped to several other concentration camps, fourteen in all, each Camp Commandant relieved to get rid of the uncontrollable lot and pushing them on. After years of bouncing around one Russian camp after another, they were finally repatriated to Spain with an almost audible Soviet sigh of relief.

I started playing basketball and baseball with the Oberena Athletic Club in my spare time. Since both sports were in their infancy at that time in Spain, my brother's and my earlier experiences made for an invaluable addition to their teams' roster. Traveling to neighboring cities on weekends to play championship games in both sports was always a thrilling experience because, brief as they were, those outings were the first taste we had of being away from home. I don't recall winning many important championship games but I clearly remember feeling delighted at the camaraderie with older team members and, even more important, being on our own for the first time in our young lives.

I met Tio José Urreaga[13] when he came to Pamplona one fall day of 1948 to visit family and friends. During his stay, he popped in the hardware store to meet and talk with his cousins from the Philippines. I suspect the real motive of his visit was to gauge my knowledge of English. As I was to later discover, that was one of my more valuable hidden assets.

During his visit, I learned about Tio José's interesting

---

[13] Son of Tio Francisco Urreaga, who was instrumental in bringing Dad to the Philippines forty years earlier to work for Ynchausti y Cia., later renamed Elizalde y Cia.

background. He'd been educated in an English Prep school in Shanghai before coming to Spain, where he played goalie for Osasuna, the local soccer Club. When the Civil War broke out, he made Lieutenant in the Tercio de Montejurra, a tough Navarran regiment that was shortly to assault and take Bilbao. It was during that military operation that he succeeded in keeping Jose Luis Aznar, a Bilbao shipping tycoon, from being executed by a Communist firing squad. In gratitude, Aznar offered him an important position in his Shipping Company when the war ended, an offer Tio José promptly accepted.

It was during that visit to Pamplona that Tio José invited me to work for his Company in Bilbao. As a Yankee catcher later famously said, "It was *déjà vu* all over again." Tio José's dad had offered my dad an analogous job opportunity almost 40 years earlier, an offer that would change dad's life forever. The lure of a promising job to work elsewhere made me giddy with anticipation. So thrilled was I by the prospects of becoming independent at the tender age of 17 that I couldn't wait to get to Bilbao. I was really ready to see the world.

Chapter 5

Bilbao

.the days of our youth are the days of our glory;
and the myrtle and ivy of sweet two and twenty
are worth all your laurels, though ever so plenty."

Lord Byron

My first impressions of Bilbao were dismal. It was drizzling when I got out of the bus and the smoggy, suffocating atmosphere that hit me in the face was utterly unpleasant. People weren't even conscious of the concept of air pollution those days or that industrial smog was noxious to one's health. Indeed, it was about that time that the English were starting to complain about London's "pea soup," the foul smog they had to live in.

The deadly fumes spewed by heavy steel mills, a busy shipbuilding industry and countless chemical factories on the suburbs of town, mingled with the constant drizzle to soot-stain every building in the city. Only God knew what it did to the inhabitants' lungs. I soon discovered that Bilbao sported the unfortunate sobriquet of *"el bocho,"* or "the hole", which it indeed merited, hemmed in as it was between the Nervión River and the surrounding hills. Bilbao was a truly unattractive and unhealthy place to visit, let alone to live in, but health and aesthetics were the last things in my mind when I started life there.

A taxi took me to Gregorio de la Revilla 2, the address of a boarding house the Aranas[14] had suggested, one of the brothers having boarded there years earlier. After walking up two flights of steps and ringing the doorbell, Doña María, the owner of the boarding house, welcomed me in. She was a short, white haired lady, with a large mole on her cheek, a slight palsy tremor and an otherwise pleasant disposition. After the introductions, she informed me that one of her four bedrooms was vacant and available for rent. Room and board, I was informed, would run 27 Pesetas a day. Since I had no idea what boarding fees were going for those days, the quoted price sounded reasonable enough to someone who still didn't know what salary he'd be earning.

The lodgings were Spartan. The small living room, which served for dining, reading and relaxation, was adjoined by several single bedrooms, a small kitchen with a coal burning stove and a hot water tank above it, a small bathroom with an enameled, clawed bathtub, a dingy toilet and a small wash basin. The living quarters struck me as something Chekhov would have felt comfortable living in or writing about. But the price was right, I thought, and so I closed the deal.

Next morning, after a frugal breakfast of chicory coffee and buttered toast, I rode to work on a trolley bus to avoid drenching my price woolen Prince of Wales suit in Bilbao's persistent *chirimiri* drizzle. The Shipping Company's offices were located in a large, elegant chalet on one of the side streets of the Gran Via, the city's main artery. Aznar was a modest enterprise, as maritime Companies went, operating 40 cargo and passenger ships that plied both coastal and international waters, transporting both cargo and passengers.

I was shortly introduced to Don Vicente Babío, a friendly,

---

[14] The Aranas had lived with us in Iloilo the last days of the war and had sailed back to Spain a year before we did.

middle aged gentleman in charge of the Regular Lines Department, to which I'd been assigned. I couldn't help noticing the respect shown him by the other employees and soon discovered the reason for such deference: a lawyer by profession and noted for his expertise in Maritime Law, Babío had studied in London for his Ship's Captain's degree, once serving as a distinguished professor in the Company's Tall Ship used for training future Officers. I felt privileged to work under him, not just because he was a patient and understanding boss but because he turned out to be a father figure for me, a young stranger in an intimidating land.

I was introduced to the other employees in our immediate group, each with his distinctive foibles and idiosyncrasies. Alfonso Migoya, the most peculiar of the lot, was a graying lawyer who worked the passenger end of the business. He never took his Bar exams because of the many years, he said, he'd lost serving in Franco's Army, both before and during the Civil War. *"Cinco años de mili,"* he'd brag sotto voce to anyone who'd listen, while pulling a lower eyelid down with a forefinger, to apprise his audience of the fact that he'd been there before, wherever "there" was. The first thing he used to do on sitting down at his desk every morning was to wrap his hands around both ends of his typewriter's roller pretending to be gunning his Montesa, while accompanying the mime with a loud, throaty roar emulating his motorcycle's 125 cc engine.

Tere Urrutia was an engaging young lady who performed efficient secretarial work in the Passenger Dept. Not being as well endowed as her cousin Blanca across the hall, in Accounting, she tried to make up for the shortfall by wearing tight, revealing sweaters to highlight her lemon drop breasts. Excited by the landscape, the young blades around her sounded her out with risqué jokes, which Tere took in with prudish equanimity.

Julio Múgica was the most gregarious and fun-loving of the lot. His previous job as a detective in the local Police Dept. came in handy

79

when solving occasional passengers' passport issues. But his real job consisted in handling the cargo aspects of Regular Lines. He would collect cargo Bills of Lading, type up the ship's cargo manifest, obtain official cargo export permits from the Consulates involved and supervise the actual loading of the cargo onto our ships in port.

Hectic as that job description sounded, Múgica had a more pleasurable life outside work. For him, as for most men in Bilbao, "*poteo,*" or barhopping, was a daily after-work sport. That activity used to go on until suppertime, usually around ten o'clock in the evening. Disgruntled wives complained about their tipsy, late-arriving husbands while local oncologists drooled at the increasing number of cirrhosis cases among the male population.

Múgica was a great raconteur who enjoyed telling funny drinking stories. I still chuckle at the one about the time he and Papis, a drinking buddy, got smashed at an out-of-town party, jumped on an unattended steam roller they found as they left the party that dawn, and taxied it home as best they could, all dressed up in their tuxes. That must have been a sight to behold. Unfortunately, they tipped the unwieldy contraption into a ditch and had to stagger the rest of the way home on foot.

I suspect that cloudy skies and the almost daily *chirimiri* drizzle were the main cause of people's depression, which, in turn, accounted for their heavy drinking. A pathetic, human interest story related to drinking sticks in my mind. Ercoreca, in Aznar's Coastal Shipping department, was working peacefully early one morning at his desk when, suddenly, two burly men dressed in white uniforms walked into his office, strapped a strait jacket on him and dragged him out, kicking and screaming, to a waiting ambulance. Weary of his drunkenness, his wife had sought legal authorization for his drying out in an insane asylum.

Looking sober and quite dried out, Ercoreca turned up a couple of months later with some wild stories about his stint at the asylum. The funniest was the one about his first night at the dinner table. A certifiably crazy inmate, who happened to be sitting across from him, mistook his masticating jaw's motion for mumbled threats. The loony stood up and threatened to punch Ercoreca's lights out. After several similar nightly threats, Ercoreca decided to beat the crazed inmate to the punch. Getting up first, he grabbed the would-be aggressor by the lapels and pushed him back violently. This so surprised the nutty inmate that it put an end to his dinner threats.

His stories about the inmates' howling and carrying on during nights of full moon confirmed something I had suspected all along. One of the inmates was convinced he was a reincarnation of Napoleon, complete with hand-over-tummy stance. Still another kept punching the palm of his hand with a forefinger, swearing it'd go through, one of those days.

Ercoreca looked pretty subdued when he came back from the loony bin. One couldn't help but feel sorry for the bloke and his erstwhile drinking problems, even sorrier still for his estrangement from his wife after her failed attempt to put him away permanently. There were no divorces then but I suspect that their case would have been a likely candidate.

My work in Regular Lines consisted mostly in handling correspondence with our international agents on diverse business matters. At first, Babío would correct my phraseology but I soon got the hang of it and started writing letters on my own, with an almost professional flair. Certain pro-forma acronyms like "q.l.b.m."[15] at the tail end of each business letter never ceased to amuse me.

---

[15] Short for "Que le besa la mano", which translates into "who (respectfully) kisses your hand"

More intriguing still was the way correspondence records were kept. Hilario, one of the Company beadles, laid each of our typewritten letters between a damp rag and a blank page of a big leather-bound tome. He'd then press the lot under a rotary press, giving the wheel a mighty twist to ensure that the information was properly transferred. A copy of the letter was more or less successfully imprinted on the tome's onion skin page but the letter itself emerged utterly wet and rumpled, its contents barely legible because the running ink had hopelessly smudged its text. This was, of course, eons before computers or Xerox copiers came to Hilario's rescue.

Handling cargo claims came easy, although some of them, like the few General Average[16] cases, were fairly daunting and drawn-out affairs. But even those were made tractable by purposely delaying answering claim letters, a tactic which inevitably led to an "In" basket teetering threateningly over my work desk. One thing that baffled me about Lloyd's of England, who insured some of our claims, was their quick response to our settlement requests. Babío explained that British gentlemen tacitly believe that if we had to have paid the original claim up front, then everything must have been on the up and up, which explained their swift payments, no questions asked. British fairplay at play, what?

During busy sailing periods, I'd give Migoya a hand with booking passengers to South and Central America. They were mostly emigrants from Galicia and Asturias in search of a better life elsewhere. I was always troubled when watching some dear old lady dig into her tattered handbag for perhaps the last of her life savings to pay the 6000-

---

[16] In Maritime Law, the owners of cargo spoiled because the transporting vessel had to be deliberately flooded in port to put out an on-board fire, have to contribute to the cost of restoring the ship's damages in proportion to the value of their cargo..

Peseta passage fare to an unknown land.[17] I was always amused to read some of their responses in the "Profession" blank of the passenger application forms, with answers such as *"Su sexo."* Some responses, like *"Sus labores,"* were less bedroom-explicit, more pots-and-pans flavored. Those, you see, were the good old days when feminism wasn't even a glint in women's eyes.

Alfonso Bravo, a retired Merchant Marine Captain, was head of the Company's Claims Department. Although he probably resented my occasional interloping into his job by handling petty claims in our Regular Lines Department myself, he was too dignified to show his displeasure. Bravo developed into a claims expert and handled all the important claims with unquestioned thoroughness. I'll never forget overhearing one of his phone conversations with an exporter's lawyer, complaining about his pilfered cargo,

> *"Testigo presencial del hecho material no existe,"* he'd assert with ex cathedra finality. *"Ahora bien"* he'd conclude," *el hecho cierto y concreto es que el bulto cayó al agua,"*

attributing the loss to a less onerous accidental spill rather than to pilferage by ship personnel. Whatever his motive, Bravo's rotund statement must have left the lawyer perfectly speechless.

One of Bravo's other quaint aphorisms was his play on words of a popular Spanish expression: *"Te doy la razón"*, which he'd twist into another of his pompous dictums: *"La razón ni se da ni se quita; se tiene!* Anyone could see that there was no possible riposte to that contusive argument.

Some of the tougher claims Bravo had to handle were complaints

---

[17] Eventually, when I lived in the United States, I would come across the progeny of some of these immigrants. Their parents had done fairly well in the New World.

about the unruly behavior of drunken Scandinavian sailors on ships consigned to us, who, upon returning to the ship after a night out in the town's red light district, staggered up the gangplank, confronted the challenging *carabineros* and unceremoniously tossed them overboard.

There was another Alfonso in the Company; this one, Alfonso Palacios, son of a well known winemaker, who worked for Aznar's Ship Maintenance Dept. Being of the same age as I, we hit if off from the start. His sharp Basque beak and a touch of strabismus didn't do much for his love life, but he was nonetheless sociable and fun loving. One weekend he invited me to ride on his Biscooter[18] to visit one of his father's wine cellars in Elciego, Alava, and taste some of their delicious white Diamante wine. When we got there, we were so engrossed in wine tasting that we didn't realize it had gotten dark outside, too late now to drive back to Bilbao. So we decided to sleep on the floor of the wine cellar, leaning our heads against the vats. The combination of fumes from the fermenting casks and our serious degustation of their wares left us with a horrible headache when we woke up next morning. We somehow managed to drive the 125 km. back to Bilbao safely the next day.

José Aguirre, an inmate at Doña Maria's boarding house was a young, ne'er-do-well roué studying for his Captain's degree at the local Merchant Marine Academy. He'd party everyday and come home drunk every night, which gave Doña María untold grief. He would on occasion borrow his father's Harley to give his girlfriends a spin around town in its side car. Once, at a loss to translate the Spanish noun *buque* (ship) into English in his final language verbal exam, he glibly replied:

---

[18] A low-slung, noisome four-wheeled vehicle with an underpowered lawnmower engine, representative of the dawning of the industrial age in the post war Spain of the early 50's.

"embarkation," directly translating from the Spanish *embarcación*. His teacher's response was fulminating: *"Sí, descojonation! Siéntese!"* The accompanying failing grade forced Aguirre to go back to sailing the Aznar ships as a lowly Second Officer.

Assigned to passenger ship duty plying the Central American route, Aguirre reverted to his Don Juan proclivities, managing to impregnate several young passengers on different trips. Irate relatives were invariably waiting for him on his next stopover to enforce the proverbial shotgun wedding in Havana, La Guaira and Barranquilla, ports on which he, obviously, couldn't safely go ashore. Irate letters started arriving from the Cuban, Venezuelan and Colombian consulates in Bilbao, demanding that Officer Aguirre be apprehended and brought to justice for his peccadilloes. Fortunately for José, his uncle Garibi, happened to be the overseer of all of Aznar's ships' Officers. He ironed things out and that was the end of that unsavory affair. It also, incidentally, was the last we saw of José Aguirre.

Sexual deviance was a serious offense those days in Bilbao. Long before the quaint "Don't ask, don't tell" rule of a latter day code of military conduct, homosexuals were simply shoved into a train and perfunctorily deported from town whenever apprehended *in fraganti delicto*. Another quaint but unspoken gentleman's agreement was invoked when a young man got his girlfriend pregnant; he was honor-bound to marry her or face the wrong end of an irate father's shotgun.

Daily visits to the U.S. Information Services library across the street from work kept me away from the *poteo* temptation. That was my first acquaintance with old American Classics such as Thomas Wolf, Michener, Dos Pasos, Sinclair Lewis, Hemingway, Steinbeck, Frost and Dreiser. It was a joyous discovery. My early meager salary forced me to make ends meet by giving English lessons to struggling Engineering students. One of them, José Ramón (Poli) Urquiza, took off for Cuba shortly after graduating, to work for Batista and then Castro, I ignore in what capacity.

The only family I had in Bilbao was Tío José's. He and his wife Mariví took me in as if I was another son, and I cherished their warm affection and hospitality. They already had two children, Vicky and Agus, and a third on the way. When Verónica was born, I was flattered to be asked to be her godfather. I was usually invited to dinner at their house every Sunday, where I was regaled with their usual Sunday fare: a delicious Paella accompanied by the best Rioja wines, topped by a Cuban cigar, coffee and a postprandial. I didn't realize at the time just how much I needed that nourishment, considering Doña Maria's Spartan fare.

Most enjoyable were the weekends at their stately chateau in the beach at La Arena during the summer. On sunny days, we enjoyed playing soccer and swimming in the beach or hiking up the nearby hills. When the weather turned cloudy or drizzly, we'd play endless games of Mus indoors and listened to records of American music which Tío José would bring back from his trips to the States. Occasionally we'd have outside visitors, the most peculiar being an acquaintance of theirs, Monsignor Valero from Valladolid, who'd utter rotund pronouncements like: *"Realmente, verdaderamente, esto es!"* feeling greatly relieved after planting that little halberd in Flanders. Every Sunday we'd all trundle over to the chateau's chapel and attend Sunday services, with Don Estanis presiding. A few years later, rumors started flying about some of his extracurricular activities with a local wench, a peccadillo that cost him his robes... and us our sermons.

I always enjoyed fishing baby squid *jibiones,* with Chencho, a local fisherman and Tío José's caretaker. His technique intrigued me; he'd row the boat out to sea, drop a line with a dozen hooks attached all up and down it, with a weight and a small white cloth dangling from its bottom to attract the squid. After the requisite number of tugs, he'd pull up the line and harvest a dozen snared tiny squid with every cast, all of which went into the scrumptious *calamares en su tinta* dish we'd eat for

86

supper that night.

The summer fiestas held on the Chateau's patio were always fun. We'd dance to the cacophonous plinking of guitars, thumping of base drums and out-of-tune tooting of trumpets and trombones until everyone got either too soused or too sleepy and had to call it quits. The Goldaracena sisters, nieces of Tia Mariví and regular summer guests at the Chateau, danced their hearts out on those fiestas. Both of them were good sports and a lot of fun.

Always the incorrigible matchmaker, Tia Mariví once whispered in my ear that one of those nieces, also named Mariví, had a warm spot in her heart for me. Though a little on the plump side for 17, she had a pretty face and a teasing disposition. I took her out on a couple of dates after that, but promptly dropped her when she refused to even hold hands with me, let alone, God forbid!, be pecked on the cheek. Most Spanish women of the time played just a little too hard to get.

There were other good lookers in Bilbao, however, some of whom I eventually got to know and date. Begoña Páramo was one of my first such dates. She was svelte and elegant, with fine, aristocratic features. She and her stunning sister, Carmen, would double date Jimmy Hicks, a neighbor of mine, and me. Things went swimmingly at first until Begoña started expecting a more meaningful (i.e. married) relationship. I was too young and impecunious to even think about such serious liaisons. Noticing my reticence, she dropped me like the proverbial hot potato. Being my very first love affair, I was pretty hurt.

 Nere Eguía soon came to the rescue. She was as young as I, and perhaps, just as romantic. Her hazel eyes were expressive, her lips sexy, and her conversation intelligent. We enjoyed each other's company immensely, frequenting movies, swimming at the beach, and dancing in different dance halls. She was the very first girl I ever kissed, and the experience thrilled me greatly. But, as usual, every doubloon had its dross; I still remember the faint taste of garlic in her mouth when we kissed, but promptly dismissed the oddity, attributing it to the sine qua non of every Spanish kitchen.

I eventually became leery of taking our affair any further than the kissing and the cuddling. As in all those early forays into love, I felt hopelessly unprepared to offer her, or anyone else, a definite, long term vow. After all, I was only 20 and a long way from being able to provide anyone a decent living. And so it was, that as in all those early flirting sorties, I eventually had to cool my ardors and pull back to a less romantic stance, and, of course, a less exciting life. I'd like to blame that reticence on an overdeveloped sense of responsibility but the truth was simpler; I was still too immature to proceed with all sails to the wind.

I'd spend some summer weekends in the Arana's summer home in the coastal town of Canala, not far from the notorious Guernica. Other than swimming in the inlet and playing Mus at the local bar with some of the local codgers, summer vacations there were pretty bland and sedate affairs. The only excitement happened whenever the town's only good-looking and healthily-endowed young lass showed up at the bar. The hamlet's blades would become instantly aroused, discreetly ogling and lusting after her. Being of a marriageable age and looking for someone more promising that the local yokels, she ignored everyone in sight with haughty disdain. There was a Spanish saying at the time that men's graying temples were a sexual attractant to women, simply because graying sideburns denoted someone old enough to be well heeled and able to provide women their longed-for security, i.e. marriage. *Cochino dinero*, the yokels concluded, and went back to their Mus.

Bilbao had its share of good looking girls. I remember Conchita Sanz, a hard to get stunner for whom I'd suffer through endless novenas in the Church of Indauchu just to be near her[19]. Then, there were the weekend visits to the home of my guitar-playing friend Chelucas Velasco. He strummed the Spanish guitar passably well and tried

---

[19] Where was Burigotto when I really needed him!

teaching me the art. But it was all just an excuse to be near his good-looking, but unresponsive sister, Marisa.

And then there was Maruja Oyaga, from Pamplona, who wrote one day announcing her upcoming visit to Bilbao. Having admired her from afar when I was in Pamplona, I was tickled by her visit and took her out dancing a couple of evenings, enjoying her good looks' and knowledgeable conversation. But she was my brother's belle at the time and that was as far as I got. Maruja grew up to be a buxom, good looking woman who eventually obtained her law degree and, later, even got elected Mayor of Pamplona. One afternoon, presiding a bullfight in that capacity during San Fermin, the young, drunken blades in *sol*, took one look at her in the President's parquet box and started chanting "*Qué buena estás, María...*" a lewd salutation she, naturally, enjoyed.

My brother Luis had just finished his degree in Business at a College in Pamplona when Tio José offered him a job in Aznar's Ship Brokerage Dept. He, as I, was elated at the offer and didn't waste any time hopping on the bus for Bilbao. We shared a room in my boarding house and he adapted nicely to life there. We slowly regained our earlier sense of camaraderie and got to know each other far better than ever.

Luis worked directly under Tio José and enjoyed his job from the first day. As fluent in English as I, he soon learned the ropes of international cargo canvassing and ship brokerage. He shared with me some of his coworkers' foibles, one of which still makes me chuckle. It was about Jesus Babio, brother of my boss, a wizened old holier-than-thou manager in his department. One day he got all bent out of shape when the Captain of an American freighter consigned to us wired on the eve of his ship's arrival in port, requesting we book a whorehouse for a week in the city's red light district, for his crew's R&R while in port. He further requested that it be outfitted with at least 20 girls and three male homosexuals. Babío made haste to refer the unsavory matter to the American Consulate, demanding that the Captain be reprimanded for his cheek.

Having been playing basketball in Pamplona all along, Luis' six foot-plus height made him an ideal center for any team. He didn't take long rounding up a handful of local young men who'd played High School basketball in the Philippines, and started a team in Bilbao. I, of course, was the other founding member of the team. We named it *Aguilas*, in memory of the Blue Eagles team of Ateneo, in Manila.

Our teamwork and coordination soon paid off. There were only five of us when we first registered as a 3rd. Division contestant in the National Basketball Association. The Escolapios High School was happy to sponsor us and let us use their courts and locker room facilities. The priests and students there were very enthusiastic and would come cheer us at every game. That first year was quite challenging, considering there were only five of us, with no substitutes to fall back on. Despite our travails, we managed to win every single game we played those first couple of years, eventually earning our way up to 2nd. Division, in the National League.

It was about that time, one Easter, when Dad started feeling puny. It was early 1952 when he first started feeling queasy in his stomach. He came to see a specialist in Bilbao, who confirmed that he had contracted stomach cancer. He was only 62. Sent back to Pamplona to be operated on, all the surgeon could do was sew him back up and send him home to die. It was a terrible blow for everyone, especially Mom, who was only 45 at the time and beginning to enjoy life in the new chalet they had moved into, in *Media Luna*, a choice location overlooking the Arga valley. I couldn't help wondering about all those cigars he used to smoke in his younger years, fourteen a day, he claimed, but that was long before cancer was definitely linked to smoking.

Dad passed away surrounded by family at dawn in early June that year, only a couple of months after his first symptom of trouble. It was fulminating. My greatest regret was not having been closer to him all those growing up years. I vowed to be more accessible to my own children when I had them, a concept then foreign in a land of stand-offish Patriarchy.

Chapter 6

Africa

Servía en Oran al rey un español con dos lanzas
Y con el alma y la vida a una gallarda africana,
Con quien estaba una noche cuando tocaron al arma.
Luis de Góngora

Shortly after Dad's passing away, I received my orders from the Draft Board. I was slated to join the Spanish Army in about half a year. Following the luck of the draw used in those selections, I'd been assigned to serve in a Company of the Chemical Warfare Division, attached to the Spanish Foreign Legion in Ceuta, the northernmost city of Africa.

Selective Service laws at the time exempted all firstborn sons of widows from military duty but I chose to disregard that exemption and go to Africa, anyway. The lure of the unknown was too strong to pass up. Besides, it would be my chance of paying the Moors back for their invasion of Spain thirteen and a half centuries earlier. I was 21 then and ready, once again, to take on the world.

Being drafted into the Spanish Army during the early fifties was like waking up among Pancho Villa's rabble, in dubious pursuit of Pershing. Assignment to Africa only compounded the hallucination, the nightmare unfolding in living color when I boarded the train in Pamplona that would take 2½ days to cross Spain before arriving in Algeciras, the southernmost Spanish city. A ferry took us across the Strait of Gibraltar to Ceuta, and although the crossing only took half an hour, the seasickness around me almost made me sick.

Most conscripts were dazed after undergoing the usual emasculating rites of delousing, shearing and serializing at the Recruit Center. Things improved somewhat after we were trucked to our outfit, a small fortified chalet literally on the very northern tip of Africa with the unlikely name of Torremocha, located at the foothills of Mt. Hacho, the Atlas Range's last burp.

Our group of thirty recruits and as many resident veterans was commanded by a mostly absentee Major, a wily Captain, an aging Lieutenant, a shady Warrant Officer and two ornery Sergeants who kept everyone under control, mostly by violent means. We were unceremoniously dumped in the barracks, assigned bunks, and ordered to put on our fatigue jumpsuits and espadrilles. We learned about our first camp assignments, mostly, degrading chores like latrine duty, de-bugging the barracks and keeping the place passably neat and tidy. Sergeant Patiño made sure we knew who the boss was around there by liberally striking the insubordinate among us with the back of his hand, accompanying his violence with a string of unrepeatable expletives.

Life soon settled down to the numbing routine of boot camp The tantalizing thing about being stationed on the very southern pillar of Hercules was the proximity of Gibraltar, its northern counterpart in Iberia, so near and yet so far. We were staring at a long 2-year period of service ahead of us and quickly learned that adaptation to military life demanded some sort of mental winding down, a deliberate dimming of the upstairs lights to help one's vision adapt to the onrushing darkness. Hibernation of the mind was a survival mechanism that demanded instilling intellectual somnolence.

There was one among us, however, for whom conscription was like dying and going to heaven. In one of the Spanish mountain ghost towns of Valladolid, where this country bumpkin was born and raised, nights must have seemed long and dreary for those who, like him, never even suspected the existence of television sets or telephones, let alone electric lights to read by - if one had the misfortune of being literate. The days must not have been much cheerier, having to grub for bread in the scrawny glebe under an unforgiving Castilian sun, with no more excitement than the occasional wayfarer describing exotic fruits like bananas and pineapples, leaving them to wonder what these mysterious fruits looked or tasted like.

Army life must have been exhilarating for 'Valladolid', for that was the name he now went by, even if it meant having to spend sleepless nights wading through disconcerting Army manuals and having to memorize all those archaic codes of military conduct. The one that intrigued him most was the obscure rule that stated: *"On entering an abode in occupied territory, the Spanish soldier can only demand three things: water, salt and a seat by the hearth."* Fancy, he must have mused, asking for salt and getting it!

There was not a dull moment in those short boot camp weeks for the rest of us. Being furnished pre Civil War equipment, target practice and grenade launching exercises were challenging, if not downright daunting. The rifles we were issued were 30- caliber WWI Mausers whose rough handling over the years had resulted in a definite sway in their barrels, making successful target practice more a thing of imaginative compensation than of true marksmanship. I somehow managed to master my swayback weapon to earn, early on, a marksmanship award.

The Italian Lafitte concussion grenades were a little more exciting. Being relics of the Spanish Civil War handed down over the humid years, their ribbons - which were supposed to completely unfurl to set off the fuse and detonate the device at a safe distance- never fully unrolled, or did so prematurely, resulting in either duds or nearby hang fire detonations. To prevent losing recruits in training exercises, we were forced to safely launch the grenades in a prone position from a cliff's edge, thus allowing any premature blasts to fly by us harmlessly.

I had a fortunate hiatus in the middle of boot camp. I volunteered to play basketball with the Benoliel team, the local civilian champions. The Commanding General of the Protectorate, a basketball fan himself, soon noticed me and ordered that I be relieved of further basic training duty and join the Benoliel team in their upcoming National Championship games in Santander, northern Spain. The day before I left, I requested my Company Captain to authorize a one-week extension of my stay in the Peninsula so that I could run the bulls in Pamplona during San Fermin. Being from Navarre herself, his wife made sure that I was granted the request.

Everything went as planned; after the basketball championship was over I enjoyed the fiestas in Pamplona. Matters deteriorated after that. Not content with a week's extension of my stay in Spain, I made the mistake of wiring the General requesting a further extension of my visit, alluding to some cooked up medical reason. The response from the General's Office was fulminating: get your behind back to Ceuta ASAP, read the threatening telegram. No sooner had I gotten off the plane and driven to Torremocha than the guard escorted me to the barber's shop for a thorough shearing[20]. Needless to say, my buddies at camp were delighted to see me shorn, once again. They never abided my taking off on a San Fermin toot while they had to suffer through the rest of boot camp.

Boot camp was over by the time I got back and the different job assignments had already been allocated to the recruits. I was pleased to discover that I had been assigned to be the Warrant Officer's office manager, a job that suited me to a tee[21]. The cushy job gave me my own

---

[20] Shearing a soldier's hair was a favorite punishment doled out to those who flagrantly disobeyed military orders.

[21] I was granted Brevet Warrant Officer status shortly after, when our Warrant Officer was demoted and expelled for sexual misconduct.

private quarters, next to the office and away from the noisy and tumultuous barracks, with enough leisure time to go swimming in the Mediterranean practically every day.

I definitely caught the Captain's attention when I started tutoring his ten year old son in English. But what really gratified him was my ghost writing his monthly patriotic addresses to the troops, which he, incidentally, was supposed to, but never delivered. I poured it on with such gusto that he started receiving kudos from Division Headquarters when they got to read the copies of the verbiage I sent them.

For 'Valladolid,' however, the excitement of boot camp was over all too soon and life quickly degenerated into an endless string of kitchen police episodes. His social gaucheness and questionable mental baggage left room for precious few other options. But even KP was fun in the beginning, especially when chasing after terrified Moorish galley boys around the kitchen, brandishing a pig's foot.

But even that little game got stale after a while, so it wasn't long before 'Val' started looking around for odd volunteer jobs outside the kitchen, regardless of the undertaking's nature or complexity. He quickly learned that claiming expertise on the subject usually landed him the job, a ruse that was eventually to be his undoing.

Val's first sally outside the kitchen literally landed him in the coop, in charge of the Company's chickens. Their rightful guardian was off on some contrived 'death-in-the-family' furlough and 'Val', who volunteered to replace him, enjoyed the brief respite immensely. We could see him walking around the coop with a beatific smile on his face, as if in a trance, a state his feathery wards did not appear to share. The first sign of trouble came with the endless cackling, followed by egg-less mornings which the Captain's wife sorely missed. Matters deteriorated when half the coop failed to answer reveille one morning, the other listless half following suit shortly after. Somebody had forgotten to tell Val about feeding and watering the fowl. It wasn't long before he went back to peeling spuds and life returned to normal around the compound.

Val's next kitchen escapade came shortly after. The Company's mule handler had come up with an imaginative excuse for a furlough, claiming his presence was required at a sister's surprise marriage. Being the sole bidder of the usual volunteer bans, Val got the replacement job hands down. He was seen marching toward the stables with great panache.

Now, it should be noted that mules in the Spanish Army of the day came complete with pedigree and curriculum vitae and were considered to be far more valuable even than any lowly foot soldier. Shamelessly pampered and fawned over, the beasts took naturally to all the attention and learned to expect it. Somebody should have warned Val about the mule-coddling treatment because no sooner had he ambled into the stable than he was seen sailing out of it, feet first, a pair of mule hooves perfectly imprinted on his behind.

From that unpropitious moment on, the stables would remain in a constant state of upheaval, the chemistry mismatch between man and beast painfully evident. Since that mule's sole military chore in our peacetime outfit was to haul the water cart from a nearby well to the Captain's private flower garden, the beast's recalcitrance and foul disposition soon caught the Captain's attention. When, as a statement of displeasure, the ornery beast relieved itself on his prized gladioli, the Captain put two and two together and promptly ordered Val back to his pots and pans.

It was about that time that Val first started toying with the idea of going AWOL. He thought of testing the system with the Atlas tribes, especially its quaint little rule about demanding salt and water and a place by the hearth. It was only his distaste for kitchens – and, by association, hearths - that made him still his urge to abscond, deciding, instead, to bide his time.

One night, as he stood guard duty on the outpost's rear entrance, Val's eyes happened to focus morosely on the mule of his tribulations, placidly grazing in the moonlight, no more than a hundred paces away. Something in Val's reticular formation suddenly snapped, stirring him into mayhem. Emitting peals of deranged laughter, he proceeded to empty a clip of 30-caliber bullets in the general direction of the ruminating beast and was in the process of reloading his second clip when general alarm sounded in the barracks. We all rushed to the post, half expecting to ward off some Moorish assault on the ramparts.

The mule survived the onslaught unscathed, thanks mostly to Al's poor marksmanship, compounded by his warped, WWI-issue Mauser's swayback rifling. The commotion earned Val a few weeks in the brig, in solitary confinement, along with the nickname of 'Matamulos[22]', emerging from detention with the dubious assignment of KP in perpetuity. He even got to looking like a spud, after a while, the head cook making sure he didn't stray too close to the table of condiments for fear his trailing vapors would wilt the vegetables or curdle the dressing. About the only sunny interval in those otherwise dreary days for Val were his recurrent imaginary incursions into unsuspecting abodes, muttering: 'Water and salt, by damn! And you can keep the hearth, thank you!'

For the rest of us, military duty had its ups and downs. Some nights we'd dress up in our civvies and amble off for a night out in town. Our garb's quality and elegant cut soon caught the local girls' attention. But they, like their peninsular counterparts, were only interested in hitching up permanently. And so it wasn't long before we'd migrate to the tea houses in the honky-tonk section of town to enjoy the occasional belly dancers' act and the sweet, mint tea served there. There was so much Kifi and Grifa smoked in those dives that we'd emerge from them

---

[22] Mule killer

with a certain giddiness and no shortage of powerful headaches.

Then, there were the yearly show-of-force excursions to the villages where the Berbers lived in the Spanish Protectorate regions of the Atlas Mountains. The way they'd welcome our squad was always impressive; marching in single file along the path leading to their villages, we'd notice their leaders and elders, all dressed up in their best white robes, lined up along the path to welcome us. If it was getting dark and the time to bivouac was approaching, we'd set up camp at the edge of their village and accept their invitation to join them in their welcoming celebration.

They'd light a great bonfire in the middle of the settlement, around which their "virgins" would perform tribal dances in our honor. After the usual chicken repast and sweet tea, we'd all wash our hands and lips with water provided in gourds, in true Moorish fashion, before proceeding to more merrymaking. If there happened to be a Galician soldier among us, he'd whip out his miniature bagpipe and regale the audience with jaunty Gaelic tunes. I would then pull out my harmonica and play Basque drinking songs, literally mesmerizing the locals with the sounds the little gadget emitted. The last evening rite consisted in their leaders' offering us the services of their "virgins' for the night, an offer we invariably turned down knowing that venereal diseases were notoriously rampant among those people.

Other exciting activities during our stay in Africa were the bi-yearly military maneuvers we held with the Spanish Foreign Legion, to whom we were officially attached. As the Chemical Warfare group's chief meteorologist, I'd measure the ambient temperature and humidity and note the local wind velocity and direction so that our troops could proceed with the "decontamination" of the area, prior to the Legion's subsequent assault. Meanwhile, live ammunition was being fired above our heads, directed over the hill about to be assaulted.

As one of our flame throwing soldiers proceeded up the hill,

98

burning the "contaminated" terrain ahead of him, he suddenly stopped, stood up, dropped his flamethrower and came running down the hill, ashen faced, terrified by the shells whistling overhead. Rather than reprimanding him for dereliction of duty, I dropped my meteorology gear, dashed up the hill, strapped on his abandoned flamethrower and continued the simulated terrain decontamination.

Slithering up the hill, bravely ignoring the shells flying overhead while squirting fire on the grass ahead of me, I started feeling an odd burning sensation in my right leg. Looking down, I was horrified to see my pant leg on fire. The 1914 flamethrower I was using had been slowly leaking combustibles behind me, leaving a ribbon of fire that eventually caught up with my pants. In one blurring motion, I dropped the flamethrower, pulled down my pants and shrieked my way back to First Aid station for a soothing salve. I still bear the scars of that accident on my thigh to this day.

Hope for any future volunteer assignments had long since evanesced for Val when, one day, about a year after the mulicide incident, Matamulos happened to lope up to the Company's bulletin board and read, *mirabile visu!*, about a request for a brief carpentry stint. The Company carpenter was off on some contrived sick leave and there had been no volunteers for the job, which consisted in hanging a painting over the Major's hearth. Desperate to get the job done, the Sergeant succumbed to Al's insistent plea and, with no little apprehension, assigned him the job.

Doubtful of Val's aptitude for carpentry, however, the Sergeant painstakingly explained to him how one went about the job. First, he explained, one had to bore a hole in the wall; then insert a lead plug into it, and finally screw a threaded hook into the plug. Febrile with anticipation, Matamulos never got past the part about boring a hole in the wall. He, nevertheless, nodded in feigned comprehension, muttering reassuringly: "No sweat, Sarge, piece-a-cake!"

Apezteguia, the Major's adjutant, a fellow conscript and city slicker from Madrid, happened to be lolling around the Major's house that day, reading comics while the Major was out of town and his wife was out shopping, when the doorbell rang. Matamulos stood in the doorway, a magnificent pick-ax resting easy on his shoulder, a diabolical grin on his face. To the adjutant, Al must have looked the spitting image of Millet's 'Man with the Hoe', with all the Markham doomsday trimmings. His peremptory "Where's that hearth?" momentarily took the adjutant aback. Not wanting to argue with the pick-ax, he showed Al into the living room and pointed at the hearth.

Rolling up his sleeves with grim determination, Matamulos picked up the ax with both hands and laid into the fireplace with thumping authority. The adjutant gawked in awe, riveted to the floor in paralyzing fear, as layer upon layer of red brick crumbled under the onslaught. Covered with the dust of his handiwork, Matamulos had a maniacal gleam in his eye as he swung his pick ax to the rhythmic, dervish-like cadence of "One for the water, one for the salt, and one for the goddamned hearth!"

The apotheosis came to an abrupt end when the front door flew open and the Major's wife sailed into the wine-dark cloud enveloping her living room. Her eyes took in the apocalyptic scene at a glance, quickly focusing on the perpetrator of the disaster, mayhem weapon still in hand. From the corner of her eye, she caught sight of the adjutant, cowering under the kitchen table, babbling incoherently. Keeping the principal suspect in her sights, she proceeded to unload produce from her shopping bag, flinging tomatoes and lettuce heads, carrots and eggs at Matamulos, inveighing against him with a fury Hell never even suspected existed. A potato bouncing off his forehead temporarily snapped Matamulos back to reality, but the enormity of his enterprise made him quickly retreat back into his fog. As he brushed past the shrieking woman on his way out of the demolition derby, he whispered hoarsely:

"I'll take the water and the salt, lady. You can keep the hearth."

To this day, learned annals of Spanish military medicine still publish dissertations on the incident, trying to decipher just what, if anything snapped in Matamulos' mind that fateful morning in Ceuta, many years ago. The irrepressible grin on his face throughout his month-long sojourn in the Monte Hacho penitentiary cell made some investigators wonder whether all that commotion was not Matamulos' clumsy way of proving that the system could be circumvented, even in this age of TVs and telephones, bananas and pineapples. Al, after all, had managed to spend a whole month away from his confounded kitchen. Dubious though that forced vacation was, it proved to be his little personal moral triumph.

The Spanish Army has since rendered obsolete certain atavisms from its codes of military conduct. Matamulos, I suppose, is back in the Mountains of Valladolid, a bit wiser and not much the worse for wear. We know for a fact, however, that Apezteguia, the Major's adjutant, was still babbling idiocies in some padded cell, somewhere in the southern Pillar of Hercules.

As all agonic/ecstatic military experiences, the day we were discharged from the Army was memorable. As we walked out of the Torremocha chalet, I was tempted to climb up to the flagpole and retrieve the family jewels I had symbolically hung from it the day I first walked in. I repressed the urge when someone reminded me that an earlier discharged soldier had actually attempted that simulacrum only to be promptly thrown in the brig for "behavior unbecoming a soldier," instead of walking out to freedom.

 Riding the ferry across the Strait of Gibraltar on our first leg home, Arturo de la Cruz Martin, my close buddy and Company Pharmacist, invited me to bide a while with his family in Toledo. Being on the way to Bilbao and not having any pressing reason to return to work immediately, I accepted his invitation. It turned out to be an unforgettable visit.

The first thing I noticed when we got off the train was the bracken rust, red upon the plains of Castile. Toledo appeared to be a land of endlessness, of mystery, where even sleep seemed to slumber.

The day had barely flattened into noon when we got off the train but it was already hot when we took the short bus ride into town. Day's flame was all around us, it being years before air conditioned buses. Nothing seemed to disturb the sun in its molten indulgence. The surrounding hills appeared to be quiet with their thoughts of granite and their whims of fern. Out in the distance, a solitary tree drooped under the sun, as if pawing at the sky for something that was lost and, not finding it, knotted up in pain to brood for another eon.

The River Tajo was like a dumb, wet embrace on the hill where the city pondered God only knew what. Only the distant whispering of the river challenged the silence, its banks, *La Vega*, a scandal of green, an insult to the dry and barren land around.

Abruptly, the grudging slope came to an end. Just beyond *Puerta de la Visagra*, was Toledo, grave, serene, beautiful, wearing the dreamy look of forgotten days. The first things I noticed after getting off the bus and walking past Plaza Zocodovér were the narrow streets' quaint

102

and allusive names; *Judería, Alfileritos, El Hombre de la Pata de Palo*, names still evoking the olden days of the Goths' Empire, after having trounced the Romans and being themselves subdued, 400 years later, by the Moors. Its buildings seemed to lean against each other across the narrow streets, like monuments of stone's love for stone, speaking the contradictory language of tiredness and contempt of death, of time's malicious mercy which had allowed a city to defy the calendar and outlive the rotting touch of circumstance.

Somnolence was wrapped around the city and silence had grown until it had the weight of ages, so hard to lift aside. "*Genie, quelle patience!*" the French say, and I knew that *Toledanos* would have delighted in the pun: "*Patience, quelle genie!*" and given it no second thought because that genius flowed in their veins and was set in every cranny of their walls. Arturo need not have reminded me of it.

Eager to see his widowed mother and brothers, Arturo walked me to his home. It was a small walk-up apartment in one of the oldest parts of town. His middle aged mother and two older brothers were there to greet their long lost kin, delirious of his safe return. They hadn't seen him in over a year. After much hugging and kissing, Arturo introduced me as his closest Army buddy. They welcomed me warmly, as they always do strangers in Castile. I was delighted to meet such a lovely family.

Arturo was impatient to show me Toledo. Promising to be back for supper, he took me to visit El Greco's home. It was like being transported back in time. Everything in it seemed to be as he had left it, four centuries earlier. The tapestries on the walls, the baroque furniture, the loom, the canopied bed, the worm-bitten stools, the yawning kegs in the cellar – everything bespoke a placid, at times tormented existence.

The paintings on the bedroom walls were the *pieces de resistance* of the quaint abode. Hauntingly stretched out in their canvases, the emaciated saints seemed as if they were trying to reach

103

beyond the bounds of the petty, planning blood, to leave the hated, all-confining flesh. I couldn't help wondering whether it was the Cretan's yearning to pull away from the torpor of the land or if it was the mysticism of the land itself that touched some inmost chord of spirituality in him, contorting and wringing from it these personages of tortured peace

Arturo then walked me to his old pharmacy in Calle de Los Alfileritos, where he had practiced before being yanked baldheaded into the Army. There were warm hugs and noisome salutations all around, and a thousand questions about his African stint. It was fun listening to their excited exchanges, all in their distinct Castilian accent. The young female pharmacist kept ogling Arturo, who seemed to enjoy the attention. It had been a long time since he'd been among his own.

The next stop was the Alcazar, the old military fortress atop a nearby hill with a huge gaping hole in one of its walls. Government sappers had blown it out in a failed attempt to breach the fortress walls and wipe out Franco's Loyalist troops within during the Civil War. I was shown the motorcycle the besieged troops used to mill the cereal on which they subsisted for several months of siege. Most impressive of all was the telephone used by General Moscardó to talk with his son, then held prisoner by the enemy and threatened with death unless his father surrendered the fortress. Engraved in stone nearby was Moscardó's memorable response: "Give your life up for Spain, my son. We will never surrender." Someone informed me that Moscardó was awarded the Laureada[23] for his gallant gesture.

Life in Toledo that week was delightful. We'd go swimming in the mud-colored Tajo in the mornings and to outdoor movies at night. We met some of Arturo's friends and even got to take out some girls to

---

[23] A Spanish award equivalent to America's Congressional Medal of Honor.

several of their all-night fiestas. Arturo was the perfect guide all along, a proud *Toledano* who knew the City's history to heart. He was determined that I not miss a sight during my stay there.

Although the dazzle of Cathedrals and Jewish Temples was impressive, the most memorable part of my stay there was driving out to the mountains of Toledo with Arturo, and staying with his old grandmother, who lived in a cabin, all alone, literally in the middle of nowhere, living off of a small herd of goats. A confirmed nature lover, she also was a most entertaining conversationalist.

Every morning, a handful of shepherds turned up to help her milk her goats. She churned that into goat cheese, which she'd cure and later sell. Goat cheese, I believe, was her only source of income, but it seemed to suffice. I've loved goat cheese ever since and often think of the dear old lady who first introduced me to it. I was impressed by her joie de vivre, the human spirit she exuded, her toughness, her resilience and, above all, her dogged independence

The hiatus in the mountains of Toledo was a foretaste of paradise, all peaceful and bucolic. Arturo and I would hunt rabbit, and once even saw a deer come down to drink in a small lake near where we were resting. Dusk's thin vigilance was almost done when we shot our last rabbit and returned to his grandmother's humble abode. The moon had grown out of the hills like a yellow flower, and a few stunted trees stood sharp against the sky. Night slipped down the mountainside, lazily preceded by the receding light. The sober majesty of those mountains made me regret having to leave the lovely land of Castile I'd just discovered.

On my last evening in Toledo, I walked the quiet streets alone. Leaning on the balustrade of the walls circumscribing the city, I watched the gray clouds fold their silence around the old, grown mountains, too quiet-hearted to care, hushed, lost in dreams. Heaven had blossomed star by star. A barking dog lent depth to the implacable silence of the night.

The land bore witness to its awesome timelessness, of centuries of ages that had dragged to a stop long ago, deterred by some mysterious hand. All of a sudden, I understood the whole cosmic power that curled and twisted and throbbed under the pregnant earth of Spain, that surged like white music in the wind of Castile, that smoldered in the knowing silence and the sage slumber of a city that had once ruled the world and that, for that matter, still did, because Time had no value in Toledo, eternity, there, being but a sudden, yet old acquaintance.

I bade farewell to Arturo and his family the next morning before hopping on the train for Bilbao. I promised to come back and visit[24] because that brief lull in Toledo had totally entranced me and filled my heart with warmth. It was the best balm and a fitting finish for that year and a half of rugged living in Africa. Toledo had been a beautiful dream.

My old job was waiting for me, when I returned to Bilbao in mid 1954. The old hands were still there, plugging away at their old jobs. Babío thought that I'd matured enough to take on added responsibilities. Besides the old chores of handling correspondence and claims, I was given the task of reporting taxes due the Government from the Company's freight and passage earnings. I discovered that in this new endeavor, the old technique of letting claims mature worked equally well. At that time, Spain didn't have much of an IRS to hound slackers and most Spaniards took advantage of it, considering that only the fainthearted paid taxes. Skipping taxes was, hence, some kind of sport. Fairplay was definitely not part of the Spanish social ethic.

---

[24] Almost every time I've visited Spain after moving to the States, I've made it a point to visit Arturo in Toledo. We have both grown older but still enjoy reminiscing about our Army days, endlessly retelling old battles. Our wives simply roll their eyes when we get started; they've heard the stories so many times before. But Arturo and I never tire.

I didn't get to enjoy Luis' company for long after returning from the service. His draft notice came up soon after, with the added onus of having to serve in Africa, like I. He was assigned to a Cavalry unit in Melilla, another northern enclave in Spain's then Protectorate of Morocco. But, he was even luckier than I; his basketball skills soon attracted the Commanding General's attention, also a basketball enthusiast. This opened up a cushy assignment at the plush Riding Club of Melilla, where he was assigned from his very first day in the Army, skipping basic training altogether, never once having to wear a uniform. This allowed him to walk around town in his elegant civvies, dating his superior Officers' girlfriends with impunity, always relying on his connections in high places to fend off any complaints. His military duty was, in other words, a bit of a joke[25]

I, meanwhile, started toying with the old idea of revalidating my High School studies into a Spanish Baccalaureate degree in order to start University studies in Spain. By then I'd saved enough money to foot that bill. I'd have to devote some time to Calculus, Physics and Chemistry, subjects I felt comfortable with but not quite up to Spanish standards of the day. That didn't worry me too much, but extending my meager knowledge of Latin into a Baccalaureate standard was not going to be easy.

I started pulling back on my basketball practices, on my dates and my leisure reading to concentrate on getting ready for the scholastic onslaught ahead. Studying during the summer and fall evenings after work came naturally but winter in Doña María's unheated living room was more of a challenge. Having to wear a woolen overcoat and ear muffs indoors was alright but having to turn pages and write down

---

[25] Years later, in his country estate outside Madrid, Luis infuriated his retired Colonel and General tennis buddies with stories about serving in the Spanish Army for almost two years without ever once donning a uniform.

answers to math problems while wearing woolen mittens was a little awkward.

Father Goñi, the Dean of Studies at the Escolapios High School where our Aguilas team made its home base, was extremely supportive of my study effort. He not only admired our team and enthusiastically promoted the sport among his students[26], but was encouraging and helpful in guiding me along with my studies. He monitored my progress with weekly tests, always unstinting with his hints and moral support. I was honored to be one of his special students.

Although my studies forced me to slack off somewhat from my basketball practice sessions, I nonetheless continued being a member of the team. The Aguilas managed to win every game in the local 2nd. Division League and was scheduled to defend its title in a national championship game to be held in Madrid early the coming year.

I was later surprised to discover that our opposing team in the finals would be from Melilla, in North Africa, precisely the one in which my brother Luis had been playing since the beginning of his military stint there. It was a foregone conclusion that the General would give him special permission to play in the Championship game in Madrid.

Both the national and local sport presses went into overtime. The unusual event of two brothers playing on opposing teams in a national basketball Championship game made a good human interest

---

[26] We taught one of his students, Emiliano, how to play basketball and encouraged him to practice with us. Years later, Emiliano matured into the Michael Jordan of Spain's National Team.

story. Even Mom, all excited, accepted tickets for the event. She already suspected that my brother was a better player than I but would be torn between applauding for one team or the other. The press puzzled over that fine point too but it would be an easy choice for mom; she'd applaud both teams equally enthusiastically.

The event took place in the Real Madrid basketball Arena in mid 1954. The place was jam packed but Mom, being a guest of honor, got to watch the game with my sister Maite from one of the reserved boxes. One could feel the electricity in the crowd. We ourselves were tingling with more than the usual pre-game excitement.

The game was close. Luis performed magnificently in his center position while I played my usual point guard spot. The only thing I remember about that game was what I did best: my dribbling and assisting game. There were no three-point jumpers in those days and since I was never a good shooter, I stayed away from the hoop unless it was an easy layup. The game was nip and tuck until the last minute. The Aguilas finally won by two points during the overtime period. It was almost an anti-climatic ending but the two brothers provided some excitement whenever they tangled. Uncharacteristically, Mom kept her cool as she waved graciously to the flashing cameras. I know she had a good time.

It was about that time that I learned that Aznar was contemplating sending me to Paris as the Company's representative, there to make the acquaintance of the principal exporters who provided cargo for our South America liners. I was thrilled by the opportunity. I'd never dreamed of visiting Paris before but the news was an incentive to start learning French. About the only French I knew then, except for the usual greetings, was "le gorgeau[27]," a phrase Luis and I cooked up and

---

[27] Our pidgin translation into French of "gorgeous"

said loud enough so Mom could hear it and groan, complaining: *"memo, mas de memo!"*

I dropped out of basketball altogether to concentrate on my Baccalaureate studies. Other than that and my upcoming French visit, the end of 1954 was rather uneventful.

There was a young employee in Aznar by the name of Marcellin, who'd been brought up in France and spoke the language like a native. Working in Administration, as one of the Big boss's secretaries, he was eager to improve his English. We agreed to get together for an hour after work every day to teach each other his specialty language. I can't say I learned much French during those sessions, except perhaps the vocabulary to avoid in polite company, but we had a good time anyway.

Being an outdoors sportsman, Marcellin took me out on weekends backpacking up the Pagasarri or some other nearby mountain. It had snowed on one of those outlying mountains one weekend in winter, but we decided to go hiking anyway. There must have been several feet of snow on the ground when we got to the top. Since we had planned on a two-night trip and the weather threatened more snow, Marcellín decided to build an igloo. Packing the snow down and sawing ice blocks wasn't hard, but laying them down in ever decreasing circles was tricky, especially as we got to the keystone block at the very top. It collapsed on us several times before we finally got it right. It snowed outside that night but we slept snugly enough in our own igloo. I was surprised how warm it was inside. We were inordinately proud of our feat.

Chapter 7

Paris

*"Quand on est jeune, il faut aimer comme un fou;
quand on est vieux, travailler come un diable. »*
Voltaire

It was the first week of January 1955 when I boarded an Iberia airplane to Paris with Julio Tudela, our man in the Canaries. Being a world traveler with a great deal of savoir faire, I knew that he'd be a perfect guide in Paris. After registering at the Hotel Continentale in Place de la Concorde, Tudela took me to supper in a fancy restaurant in Montmartre, followed by a visit to the Nouvelle Eve, next to the Moulin Rouge, both high class cabarets in that part of town.

Everything went swimmingly at first. Over glasses of champagne, we watched the girlie show and admired the scenery. Just before the entr'acte, the maître d' stopped by with an album of photographs of the performers, asking which of them we'd like to invite for a glass of champagne at our table during the intermission. Tudela rifled through the album and, without skipping a beat, pointed at the buxom Swiss dancer he'd been eyeing all evening. I selected a brunette, not as well endowed but with a charming smile.

I don't know what got into Tudela to tell the maître d' that I was a famous Spanish bullfighter and that he was my manager. The news must have spread like wildfire backstage; not only did the two chosen girls come to our table during the intermission but all the chorus girls danced around our table during the second half of the evening show, mussing my hair with their feathers, twirling their tassels in my face, blowing me kisses and otherwise embarrassing me to distraction.

Noticing my mounting apprehension at all the unexpected attention, Tudela proposed we make a hasty retreat before the act came to a close. I concurred and we were out of there before the onslaught started. Laughing all the way to the Continentale, I explained to Tudela that I'd seen matadors in Pamplona hotels during San Fermin hounded by the town's crème de la crème girls, but didn't realize the same attention was dispensed in France. I couldn't help wondering how many times Tudela had pulled that trick on previous trips but his harebrained scheme left me feeling like the proverbial innocent abroad.

Next morning Tudela took me to the offices of Consortium Maritime Franco Americain, in 25 Place du Marché St. Honoré, and introduced me to the higher ups in the organization. Shaking hands all around, they warmly welcomed me to the Firm. Being the nephew of José Urreaga and a close acquaintance of Javier Aznar himself, didn't hurt. The aristocratic Philippe de Bouard, Babío's counterpart in the French Company, showed me around the office, introducing me to the employees I'd be working with. He suggested I transfer to the nearby Hotel Tuilleries[28], not far from work. He also suggested I enroll at the Sorbonne to learn the finer points of French Civilization, and, en passant, the French language I'd need to communicate with exporters.

Although I enjoyed the accommodations at the Tuilleries that first week, I moved to the more modest Hotel Lion d'Or nearby, shortly

---

[28] Ann and I stayed at that nice Hotel on one of our trips to Paris, years later.

after. The unpretentious hotel was located next to the St. Roch[29] Church, with historic connections to the French Revolution. That sort of cachet appealed to me. I was not totally surprised that in the more modest Hotel, I'd have to pay the concierge 25Fr. to unlock the padlocked hot water spigot every time I wanted to take a bath.

During breakfast at a nearby bar/restaurant before morning classes, I noticed several Frenchmen at the bar drinking white wine at that early hour. I remember reading a French demographer's complaints about France's having the highest incidence of alcoholism anywhere. Beating the Bilbainos at their own game made me chuckle.

The Sorbonne classes were another eye opener. Young students from all over the world were taking the same French Civilization course I was. I suspected the professor teaching my course had been awarded the Legion de Honneur for her jingoistic approach to the subject. Gaul was there long before Rome, she assured us. I resented her slighting the Canadian students' French-Canadian accent, poking fun at their rustic, non-Parisian pronunciation. Her chauvinistic Gallic superiority bothered me. It was my first whiff of French *hauteur*, which left me unimpressed.

Back at work, I got to meet some of my co-workers, among whom was Eric de Chavignac, a young man in his late 20's, who sported a crew cut and a bristling moustache, a friendly disposition and an outrageous sense of humor. We communicated in English the first few days until I gradually picked up some French phrases. Eric loved Spanish music and made it a point to take me in his Citroën *Deux Chevaux* almost every evening, first for a quick bite at the L'Epicerie bistro, then a stop at L'Escale, a small restaurant near Boulevard St. Germain, a stone's throw from Aux Deux Magots, where Peruvian

---

[29] Near where French revolutionaries ripped the first cobblestones off that street, to build barriers while bellowing their now famous "aux barricades!"

113

medical students played their native instruments and sang haunting Inca music. Both establishments being at the heart of the *Quartier Latin*, I got to know *la Rive Gauche* quite well early on.

Some days we'd eat at Chez Niko, a small Greek restaurant catty corner from the St. Germain de Près church. I remember tasting my first *dolmades* there, which I loved. We'd sit at long dining tables next to perfect strangers, once meeting a young Parisian who, detecting my American accent, grumbled about Americans being "just big boys." Piqued, I remember answering: "Couldn't it be that you Continentals are already a bit too old?"

Eric invited me several times to supper at his father Jules' flat in one of the fancier *arrondisements* in Paris. Eric admitted that their real name wasn't the aristocratic de Chavignac he went by and that his *vieux* had adopted it to avoid being tracked down for having collaborated with the Germans during the war. His confidence in my implicit silence impressed me.

My French got progressively better as the days went by. It must have taken all of fifteen days before I could finally understand the conversation around me and express myself halfway intelligently. I even started dreaming in French. Eric's encouragement helped. I was trying so hard, during that two-week learning period that I could literally feel tiredness in my brain. It reminded me of the times I'd have to translate English into Spanish and vice versa, for Tia Marivi's benefit, at Tio José's home in La Arena, when American guests came visiting.

Monsieur de Bouard was a friendly, graceful gentleman. Some afternoons, I'd ride piggy back with him on his Lambretta, weaving in and out of traffic, to meet important French exporters whom I was supposed to contact during my Paris visit.

114

Occasionally, the Company's President and his CFO invited me to lunch at some fancy restaurant in nearby Fauburg St. Honoré. I was always impressed when they pulled a card out of their wallets to select the best vintage year of a given expensive wine they were about to choose for that meal. At first, that sophistication was a bit rich for me but I learned to accept it gracefully. After all, I thought, I was their favorite client's representative.

Some days I'd eat a sandwich for lunch at le Jardin des Tuilleries, a short walk from work, with one of the Firm's secretaries, a petite Jewess named Minou who kept making eyes at me. We'd amble over to the Jeu de Pomme Museum after lunch to admire the impressionists' paintings[30] there. She later gave me a picture of herself with something written on the back. It was years later that I happened across it and read: ..."*tu a manqué quelque chose.*" That made me

wonder just what boat I'd missed by not taking her more seriously.

Having coffee at Aux Deux Magots one afternoon, Eric and I met two young students from the Sorbonne, also having coffee there. One of them was a Welsh girl named Daphne, the other a German named Helga. The latter, a girl no older than 18, had a graceful figure, beautiful blue eyes and a very friendly disposition. No sooner had we met than I forgot all about Eric, concentrating my attention on the attractive Bavarian, who corresponded with equal interest. Although neither of us knew French well enough, we somehow managed to communicate our attraction for each other. *Coup de foudre*, I believe the French call it. I had heard that German girls were

---

[30] Art transferred years later to the Musée d'Orsay.

naturally attracted to Spaniards, and I was about to test the theory.

Helga and I dated almost daily from that afternoon on. Almost in my mid twenties, I was, nonetheless, new to love, as was she. Our favorite haunts after class were the ones I'd discovered earlier with Eric. We hung out at L'Escale fairly regularly although our besotted attraction for each other made us totally oblivious to the haunting Inca music in the background. I'd occasionally visit her at Madame Tollet's apartment on Boulevard Victor Hugo, where she boarded. We'd dim the lights and dance to soft background music till late hours, holding hands and kissing to our hearts' content. Our joy and love for each other were almost unreal.

One evening, I took her out to a night club in Place du Tertre, in the heart of Montmartre[31]. It must have been three in the morning when the chansonier sang his last ballad. Most people had already left; Helga, I, and a few actors were the only ones left in the night club. Unexpectedly, someone proposed a performer/audience singing contest. Inspired by a few Sauternes, I got up on the tableau when my turn came up and sang the American ditty "Oh Susana..." which drew subdued applause from the bleary eyed audience.

It was late when we finally left the night club. We had missed the last Metro home and were just sitting there, on the steps of the Sacre Coeur, waiting for the first hint of dawn and the first metro. It was cold. Warm breath billowed in the night air as we sat close together, lending warmth to each other with thoughts of young lovers. We quoted neither Baudelaire, nor Rimbaud nor any of the other hopeless romantics, but some young and already-anonymous poet who had written words of love with haunting realism:

---

[31] near where Picasso had lived and painted in his younger years.

J'aurais voulu être un baladin,
Un trouveur, un rêveur de grands chemins,
Errant dans le matin clair…
Mais tu es venu, et je m'ai suis tu,
Ensorcelé.

In shivering hushes, we touched on heavy subjects like Existentialism and Impressionism and not a few other "isms." I remember humming haunting strains of Inca music we'd heard at L'Escale, our smoke-choked student hang-out. The bewitching Inca strains of "*Mi morena*" came bubbling up; they still haunt me with their Andean beauty to this day:

We almost froze, counting stars in the Pleiades, but *amor vincit omnia* and we made it through the dawn and into the first metro.

Eric took us both on his *Deux Chevaux* to Rouen on a business trip, a week later. The tall buildings in the port city were impressive but the big Gothic cathedral on the main square took my breath away; it was where Jean d'Arc, *la pucelle de Rouen*, was burnt at the stake.

Pointing at the spanking new derricks lining the wharf, Eric told me how the locals blamed the British for having leveled their port facilities during the war just to get rid of any postwar English maritime competition. I detected a certain Hundred-Year-War undercurrent still swirling at that late date.

My 24th birthday coincided with the graduation day of the French Civilization course. Peter Van der Heyden, son of the Dutch Ambassador in Paris, threw a graduation party for his classmates at his parents' palatial home near Bois de Boulogne. Being classmates of the young aristocratic Dutchman, Daphne, my Welsh friend, and Helga were invited to the soirée. They didn't have far to look for dates for the evening; Helga invited me while Daphne invited Franco, an Italian newspaperman with the Milan Express, who happened to own a Lancia and offered transportation for the evening.

I exchanged pleasantries with Daphne during the party, misguidedly referring to her as English. Being Welsh, she took umbrage at my gaffe. Trying to correct my faux pas, I made further small talk and asked her if she'd read Pierre Daninos' latest book *Le Carnet du Major Thomson*, then on the local bestseller list. When she said she hadn't, I proceeded to quote some of the more nuanced passages of the book[32]. She, of course, didn't appreciate that, either.

Helga and I danced till the wee hours and when the party was over, all four of us piled into Franco's Lancia[33] and headed back to our respective homes. The first snow had started to fall in the heart of Paris. Slow to react to a red light at an intersection, Franco suddenly stepped on the brakes, causing his car to hydroplane on the wet snow, ramming it into another car that happened to be crossing the intersection at that moment.

It was a hard collision and Daphne, who happened to be sitting on the front passenger seat, went sailing into the glass windshield, shattering it and severely cutting her cheek and forehead. Two young Americans, who happened to be driving by, stopped, picked us up and took us to the nearest emergency room. Daphne groaned all the way there, while I applied pressure on her wounds with a towel to keep the bleeding down. Franco, meanwhile, had gone to the nearest Police station to report the accident. We never saw him again.

---

[32] On the eve of her marriage, a naïve young Englishwoman went to her aunt for fist night marital advice. "I know it's disgusting, dear," advised the proper old bat, "but just close your eyes and think of the British Empire."

[33] The Lancia was so ancient its windshield was not equipped with unbreakable glass. It, of course, also lacked seat belts.

Helga and I spent a good hour and a half in the hospital's waiting room, waiting for Daphne to show up. She eventually did, with her head almost completely wrapped up in bandages. They had given her 200 stitches, the Doctor informed me[34].

It was three in the morning when Helga and I took her back to the nun's convent where she was boarding. The nun who opened the door almost passed out when she saw her. We brought her flowers the next morning and that was the last time I saw Daphne[35].

I'd been in Paris for two months now. My French was passable[36] and I'd met all the important exporters I'd come to meet. It was time for me to go home. It wasn't easy saying goodbye to all my friends, especially to Helga, and to the City of Light that had made my stay so memorable.

Helga and Eric came to bid me adieu at the Gare de Luxembourg, when I boarded the train to Spain. They promised to come visit me that summer, and that made parting slightly more bearable.

---

[34] Years later, Daphne wrote explaining how the French doctors had failed to detect her broken cheek bone, which had to be operated on all over again when she returned to London.

[35] Daphne had been invited to a debutante ball a month later, hosted by the Queen of England, an event she obviously had to postpone. I talked to her over the phone many years later. She graciously thanked me for taking her to the hospital that night and told me that she had married someone in the English Peerage, a descendant of William the Conqueror, no less.

[36] I met a French couple at the Hotel Loizu that summer who asked me what part of Paris I was from, a question that pleased me immensely.

Chapter 8

The Dawning

Crus amet qui nunquam amavit[37]
Pervigilum Veneris, I

The trip back to Hendaye was uneventful, except for having spent my last Franc in the dining car, leaving me with no means of proceeding from Hendaye to Bilbao. I remembered having relatives in nearby San Sebastian, where I could spend the night and borrow money for the ticket to Bilbao. Unfortunately, I couldn't remember my aunt Beatriz' married name. As a last recourse I rifled through the San Sebastian telephone directory to try to contact her. Fortunately, their family name, Aristeguieta, started with an A. They graciously took me in for the night and sent me off to Bilbao the next morning.

Bilbao was cold, blustery and drizzly in March. I lived in a daze for a while, trying to decompress from the exhilarating life of Paris and acclimate to the drab surroundings of Bilbao. Helga and I corresponded in French at least weekly and Marcellin helped me with my spelling. I spoke the language fluently enough but grammar was something else. Helga told me she'd landed a job with the Haute Couture Firm of Magi Rouf in Paris but pined for the days spent with me.

---

[37] Let those love now, who never lov'd before

She came down to Pamplona that summer for the San Fermin festivals, towing Eric and the two Tollet siblings, in whose home she boarded in Paris. While in Pamplona, I set them up at our family's chalet in Media Luna, Mom being away on a summer vacation. Rosario, the housemaid, didn't much approve of the intrusion. After several days in Pamplona the Parisians moved to a small hotel on the beach in the outskirts of Bilbao, and I was happy to show them around town.

My feelings for Helga had cooled somewhat. I supposed at first that it was Bilbao's not having the free-wheeling, laissez faire atmosphere of Paris. Helga and I parted company a week later, promising to write, which we did, but more sporadically now. Although Helga still had her eye on marriage[38], I wasn't anywhere near ready for that commitment. The grim reality that Bilbao lacked the fairy tale atmosphere of Paris must have had a damping effect on lifetime pledges of that nature. I always felt I wasn't ready for that undertaking, regardless of the level of my infatuation.

One weekend, later that summer, while staying at Tio José's chateau in La Arena, I made the acquaintance of Fan Fan, an attractive young French girl then lodging at a boarding house at the bottom of the hill. I was delighted to be able to practice my French again. But what intrigued me most about her was her visiting Spain on the off-chance of emulating Francois Sagan's main character's summer fling with a Spaniard in her *Bonjour Tristesse* bestseller. That piqued my interest. We frolicked at the beach and went on picnics on the sun-drenched cliffs overlooking the sea, and had a ripping good time together, just being our young carefree selves, lost in a typical summer fling. At summer's end I accompanied her back to Irun to catch the Paris Express, and that was the extent of my fling with the young French ingénue.

---

[38] As was her mother's, in Karlsruhe, who promised us a Porsche as a wedding gift if we followed through.

Back at work that fall, life reverted to its humdrum monotony. I had dropped out of basketball altogether and spent most evenings working on my Baccalaureate's final exams. I remember escorting Tia Mariví one evening to a Chopin concert by Nijinski, a renowned Polish pianist. His playing brought back memories of Mari Blanca's piano renditions of Chopin's Mazurkas, Berceuses and Polonaises. The music flowed over me as it once did, like white music in the dark night of war. I can still remember how the Japanese soldiers patrolling the street below would stop to listen to her angelic music.

I went to Pamplona to spend Christmas vacations with Mom that year. Unbeknownst to me, she had invited Jac Chambliss'[39] daughter, Ann, to spend Christmas with us in Pamplona. Having just turned 20 and keen on adventure in a new land, she accepted the invitation.

I picked her up at the train station in Pamplona the day she arrived. She looked slightly bewildered at first but I admired her spunk for visiting a foreign country without knowing more of its language than "*hombre*" and "*sombrero*." It didn't take me long to realize that she was different from any other girl I'd met before. She was young and physically attractive but there was something else: she was intelligent, well read, very proper, in an English sort of way, with a haunting smile and a sweet, feminine voice with a southern accent, traits I never noticed in any other girl I'd met before. It came as no surprise to realize that I was falling hopelessly in love with her. For some happy quirk of fate,

---

[39] Jac Chambliss – one of our liberators during the war – had corresponded with Mom for ten years running and had recently announced that his daughter, Ann, was in Scotland on her Junior Year Abroad program. Mom, the eternal schemer, didn't hesitate to invite her to spend Christmas with us. It had all the prospects of one of those pre-arranged Chinese weddings in the making.

the attraction was mutual.

Evenings, Ann and I would take Beltza, Mom's German shepherd, out for a walk around the Media Luna, as an excuse to hold hands and enjoy the romantic overlook of Pamplona's Rochapea valley below, with the Arga languidly flowing through it. The nights were cold but our hearts warmed to the excitement of two young lovers discovering true love for the very first time in their lives.

Christmas was special with Ann in our house. For lack of central heating we sat around a *mesa-camilla*[40] Being an Episcopalian, the Catholic midnight Mass ritual at the San Ignacio Church didn't seem too out of the ordinary for her. She enjoyed *turrón* but got sick on *yemas*. We attended the New Year Eve's party at the local Tennis Club[41], where we kissed in dark corners, more than danced.

Sometime that week, I took her to Burguete to meet grandmother Amachi. Everyone at Loizu was duly impressed by the young American, but Amachi's suspicion was aroused by her grandson's lovelorn glances at the young American. Women have a nose for such things, I always suspected. Her raised eyebrows and subsequent remark said it all. "*No podía encontrar una chica Española?* [42] "

The two- week vacation went by too fast. We promised to write and see each other again before she went back to the States. Before our

---

[40] A round table with a heavy coverlet spread over a brassier with coals burning under it to warm one's feet.

[41] Weeks later, back in St. Andrews, she surprised her classmate from Pamplona, Rosa Mari Agudo, when she told her she'd spent her vacations in Pamplona at the Lacambra's. Years later they were to become *concuñadas*, i.e. in-laws, since Rosa Mari's sister, Maite, was to marry my brother Luis.

[42] "Aren't there enough nice Spanish girls around?"

entranced interlude was over, I had pretty much made up my mind that this was the girl I wanted to marry. Even though she confessed she'd love to live in Spain, I knew I couldn't offer her the life she deserved with my meager means and unpromising future. There was only one possible solution: I had to earn a better living and, for that, I had to go to the States and obtain a degree in an American University.

It sounded like a heroic measure at the time. As it turned out, it was. It meant abandoning my job and cutting all my Spanish connections, including my family's. I had a recurring thought of the Spanish Conquistador drawing a line in the sand and asking his men to cross it with him to seek a newer world, or of Cortés' burning his ships. *Alea jacta est!* The decision was indeed made. A bright future in a promised land awaited and, with it, the prospects of marrying the first woman I'd ever truly loved.

Reminiscences of earlier prospects of life in the United States came flooding back; right after the war, I had applied for, and been admitted to the Bellarmine College Preparatory School in California, a feeding ground of Santa Clara University. Unfortunately, the plan fell through. Dad had decided that the family shouldn't split up on the eve of our planned return to Spain. I always regretted that decision.

But now, years later, I was independent and could make my own decisions. After considerable soul searching, I made up my mind. Ann's allure only confirmed my decision. All I had to do now was choose a career and a University. I was almost 25, a good seven years older than most entering University freshmen but that never fazed me. I would have the will and determination that younger students lacked. I would have the advantage of age and experience over them.

Ted Ryberg, with whom I'd been corresponding since our trip on the President Polk years earlier, came to visit me in Bilbao in the spring of 1956. He had graduated from Gettysburg College in Pennsylvania with a Philosophy major and was now studying for a Masters degree in

Library Science. He suggested I choose a small Liberal Arts college rather than one of the larger Universities, where I'd only be a number. He was, I now realize, preaching to the choir. If I was to discover America, I figured it would be from the ground up, so to speak. I had loved the United States from my earliest school years, admired her naïve, bumbling, youthful approach to life along with her awesome, leashed power, and had yearned to live there one day. In truth, I had felt more American than Spanish for some time now.

At the end of her year abroad program in June of 1956, I invited Ann to come to Spain for a short vacation in Mallorca before rejoining her family on a planned tour of Europe in July. They could pick her up in San Sebastian, giving her father, Jac, a chance to be with us again, eleven years after Iloilo.

Since it wasn't considered proper to travel alone with a young lady, I asked Mom to come as a chaperone, a proposal she gladly accepted. Ann flew into Bilbao and stayed at the Carlton Hotel that first night. She, Mom and I were asked to dinner at Tio José's that evening and it turned out to be a lovely reunion. Tio José and Mariví were duly impressed by the young American.

Next morning we took an Aviaco flight to Palma de Mallorca and stayed at a small hotel by the beach when we got there. I rented a Vespa motorcycle to tootle around the island's coast, while Mom stayed in town visiting museums and cathedrals. Ann and I had a wonderful time exploring coves and white sand beaches. Playa Magalouf was the highlight of that vacation. It was a beautiful, ten-mile stretch of sugar-white beach with nothing on it except a small stand selling cokes and sandwiches[43]. If Ann and I didn't know it before, we were now happily

---

[43] Many years later, this same beach became a wall-to-wall condominium complex. Northern Europeans had taken Mallorca by storm and the saying went that the island would sink if they built one more condominium on it.

convinced that we were utterly in love with each other. I never felt happier in my life.

Evenings, we'd go dancing at some fancy hotel's outdoor ballroom. Mom stood by in the background, discretely watching, saying nothing. I think she knew what she had wrought. I remember dancing to the French song "Enchainée," my favorite song from then on.

After a week in Mallorca, we flew back to San Sebastian where Ann's family came to pick her up on their grand tour of Europe. Our parting was sad but we had pledged our troth to each other and knew we'd meet again in the States.

After the Mallorca idyll, I wrapped up my Baccalaureate studies and took the final exams at the Escolapios High School. I passed with flying colors and Father Goñi was happy to sign my graduation diploma. The time had come to start looking for Colleges and Universities in the United States.

The United States Information Service Library near work was helpful. Ted's suggestion to limit my search to small schools, i.e. Colleges rather than Universities, was useful. I read up on each school's study programs and scholarship offerings, and requested application forms from a selected few.

Exhilarating months followed. Ann and I wrote assiduously and lived for each other's letters. Meanwhile, I tried homing in on some College before the school term started in September but there were too many schools to choose from, forms to fill and decisions to be made. Since I had missed that year's College acceptance date, I figured on making my choice with more calm and deliberation.

After several tries, I finally homed in on Gettysburg College. Not only had Ted recommended it highly but they were offering me a full scholarship from day one, which was more than any other College offered. I suspect that Ted and his friend, the College's Registrar, may have had something to do with that generous decision. The die was cast, once again, and all I had to do now was merely mark time for my planned trip to the U.S. the following spring.

I had saved enough money over the years and invested it in the Bond market, enough to tide me over the first years of College, but that little nest egg took a tumble when I unadvisedly sold my investments the very day the Suez Canal crisis broke out in October of 1956. My inexperience in market gyrations during a crisis made me take a hefty loss when the market dropped precipitously. I chalked that one up to experience and had to make do with what was left. My planned trip to the United States remained intact.

I merely marked time till the spring of the following year. Ted Ryberg, who had worked several summers as the night manager at the Beach Plaza Hotel in Ocean City, Maryland, had, for study reasons, tendered his resignation for his next summer's job and recommended me as his substitute when the hotel opened for the summer season in 1957. That suited me to a tee; it would give me a chance to acclimate to the U.S. before starting the school year at Gettysburg that September.

I prepared to sail for the United States in the spring of 1957. I had arranged passage on one of our Company's tramp vessels, the Monte Orduña, due to sail from Bilbao to New York in early May. Ted would be waiting for me in New York to drive me down to Ocean City.

Chapter 9

Coming to the United States

"I must go down to the seas again,
to the lonely sea and the sky.."

Sea Fever
John Masefield

I said my goodbyes to Luis, Tio José's family and friends at work before boarding the Monte Orduña in early May of 1957. It was the Company's only vessel leaving Bilbao that week bound for New York. I didn't know it at the time but part of that trip would turn out to be quite harrowing.

The ship was a decrepit 10,000-ton vessel, built in 1914, claiming a maximum speed of 8 knots. It was sailing on ballast, with its propeller spinning halfway out of the water even in fair weather. I was assigned the only passenger stateroom aboard and, being a Company employee and nephew of one of its Directors, I was treated with kid gloves and invited to join the Captain and his Officers in their dining room for dinner every evening.

After a brief call in Santander, we took off on our projected 12-day trip to New York. The first week of the passage was uneventful. I had plenty of time to read Thomas Mann's "The Magic Mountain," which I found heavy reading. I befriended some of the Officers on board, the youngest of whom taught me how to iron and fold shirts, a

129

domestic chore that would stand me in good stead years later. Slowly, an informal camaraderie developed between me and the Officers. I was invited to hang out on the bridge any time I wished and enjoyed looking over the shoulder of the Second Officer as he took bearings with his sextant, converting his sightings, after complex trigonometric equations, into course bearings the ship had to follow. This was years before GPS readings became available.

After dinner every evening, I'd trundle up to the bridge where the helmsman invited me to grab the helm and steer the ship, always following the required bearings on the large compass in front of the wheel. My first attempts were terrible, as evidenced by the snaky wake the half-submerged propeller cut behind us. On subsequent days however, I learned to compensate for wind and current to avoid over-steering the vessel. After a few days of casual, after-dinner 'helming', I started noticing that the ship's wake behind us was no longer snaky but straight and true. I was immensely proud of myself.

Trouble started while sailing off the Azores. A stiff wind was blowing that evening and I had difficulty keeping course, being blown by about ten degrees off it. Without consulting the helmsman, I decided to give the gale the run-around by swinging the ship a good 270° around the wind and, from there, ease comfortably back onto course. The result of that misguided maneuver was calamitous; the ship getting stuck 90° off course, stern now firmly to the wind. After trying unsuccessfully to straighten her out, I desisted and handed the helm back to the distraught helmsman who, try as he may, only managed to turn the ship and make her face the storm, still 90° off course. This sorry state of affairs continued for the next three days.

The gale soon whipped up into what felt like a full-blown mid-Atlantic storm and all the ship could do was face the storm and ride it out as best she could. The waves soon grew in intensity and the ship shuddered dreadfully every time the ship's stern rose above the water and its propellers spun uselessly in the air. That was gut-wrenching enough but what really caught my attention was the worried look on the Captain's and Officers' faces when observing the giant waves' frequency, which caused the ship's bow and stern to ride two neighboring crests while the middle of the ship sagged ominously downward, making frightful groans, as if threatening to snap the keel in two. The ship, after all, had been built 43 years earlier and should have been junked long before then.

We lost three days of travel time riding that storm. To this day, I'm not sure whether that would have happened even if I hadn't started the calamity by steering her off course. The storm eventually abated and we arrived in New York on the 25th of May 1957, 15 long days after leaving Bilbao[44].

It was late in the evening when we sailed into the port of New York. As in my arrival at Barcelona on the Ciudad de Valencia years earlier, I missed seeing the most important landmark, in this case the Statue of Liberty. As we sailed into the Hoboken docks, I was awed by the stream of traffic illuminating Riverside Drive. I couldn't help sensing that I was about to land on a promised land.

Ted Ryberg was there the next morning to welcome me, waiting to drive me down to Ocean City, Md. After the Immigration and Customs formalities, we hopped on his Pontiac convertible and tooled on down the Eastern seaboard, past Dover Delaware, and finally on to the Beach Plaza Hotel, on the town's 13th St., then practically the last large building on its northern boardwalk. It was purportedly one of the newest and finest hotels in town at the time. Ted introduced me to Mr. Kelly, the owner, a jovial Irishman with a funny sense of humor. Having been introduced as "Joe," he proceeded to call me "Joe, Joe, the dog-

---

[44] The Cunard Liners of the day used to make the crossing in 5 days from Southampton.

131

faced boy," wherever that came from.

Ted quickly taught me the ropes, which were fairly straightforward; I'd work nights, from 10:00 p.m. to 7 in the morning, type up the guest's bills, answer any phone calls, sign up late-arriving guests and generally take charge of the hotel at night. I shared a first floor hotel room with Warren Bimesteffer, whom I jokingly called "Bim-o-better." He was my age, had just graduated from a nearby College and whose summer job consisted in managing the hotel's stock room.

Ted stayed on a couple of days and showed me around the hotel. He tried to convert my eating manners from my European to American ways. It was awkward having to put down the knife after cutting the meat and shifting the fork to my right hand for eating. Equally awkward was having to rest my left hand on my lap while eating, instead of leaning my left elbow on the table. He also showed me how to operate the office's antediluvian telephone panel, with its dangling cords and plugs, as well as how to type the bills and fill out the day's log. He tried to convey Kelly's desire to turn down Jewish guests, a foible that I couldn't implement anyway, not being able to distinguish a Jew from a Christian by either name or feature.

I thanked Ted profusely when he left for school two days later[45]. He had gone well beyond the call of friendship in his many kindnesses to me, first by suggesting I apply to the right College, then picking me up in New York and driving me down to a summer job he had lined up for me, introducing me to the owner, and finally, showing me the ropes of my summer job. That was my first real brush with American kindness and generosity. I knew I was among a kind and gentle people.

―――――――――――

[45] Although we kept up a correspondence, I was not to see Ted again until my wedding day, three years later, where he would be my best man.

Slowly, tentatively, I started picking up on the local idioms and turns of phrase. That summer at the Beach Plaza served as the greening of a Spaniard and I enjoyed every minute of it, from the ease with which I slipped into my job to the nice people I met. Dealing with the guests at night sometimes brought on awkward moments. There were the occasional cultural disconnects, the funniest being the time I suggested the Navy base in Norfolk when asked by a guest where he could get a 'sub,' a disconcerting reply which startled my interlocutor. The food in the dining room was the haute cuisine the Hotel offered. But I soon tired of roast beef, lobsters and Maryland crab cakes, and drifted to the downstairs cafeteria for more mundane Smithfield ham sandwiches and plain old hamburgers with milk shakes.

Warren was a revelation. Having bumbled from one College to another playing College football, he seemed to admire my "foreignness," insisting on teaching me the fundamentals of American culture. Of a Methodist persuasion, he claimed one didn't really have to go to church, being able to commune with God anywhere in nature. I found the period songs he sang quite amusing[46]. Once, he drove me all the way up to Baltimore in his old Ford to meet his mother, a lovely lady of German ancestry who thought the world of her Warren. It was all very American and very touching.

My arrival in Ocean City coincided with Ann's week of final exams in Connecticut College. She, nonetheless, decided to catch the train to Baltimore for a quick visit with me there. I took a bus to the train station and met her as she came off the train. She looked just as pretty as I remembered and I fell in love all over again. It was a joyous reunion, even though we knew it would be a short one.

---

[46] "..Cause that crazy ol' sun has nothin' to do.." and, of course, Harry Belafonte's jewel, "Boo-boo dad": "Shut your mouth, go to bed, Papa look a boo-boo dad, Oh no, my daddy can't be ugly so."

We were so excited at seeing and talking to each other again that, much to our chagrin, we inadvertently strayed into the station's Lady's room. We ordered lunch at a nearby Irish pub but we were so engrossed in conversation that we didn't touch our food. Sooner than we thought, it was time for Ann to catch her train back to Connecticut. Frustrating as that short visit was, it filled a void and soothed a longing hard to explain. As we kissed goodbye, she promised to visit me again that summer.

Back in the hotel, I noticed that the kitchen was staffed only with black people, the Chef loudly proclaiming to be "Bull-shittin' Eddie from coast to coast." I remember once choosing an ice cream flavor by pointing at different offerings while unthinkingly reciting "eenie, meenie, miney mo, catch a nigger by the toe.." in front of the sweet old black lady dispensing the ice cream. I can still taste the blood on my tongue from belatedly biting it.

And, of course, how forget Miss Pearl, the little old lady in charge of the hotel's cleaning crew, always complaining about her health, always moaning: "If I could only find that Elton!" Trying to be helpful, Warren and I would strike out in search of Elton, always surprising him hiding in the same vacuum cleaner closet, fast asleep on his feet, sometimes even softly snoring.

The waiters and waitresses in the hotel's dining room were all white College kids, a nice bunch of fun-loving people, all younger than I. I remember joining them occasionally at their beach parties, where lobsters and shrimp were cooked over coal briquettes in a deep hole dug in the sand, covered with banana leaves and sand, and left to cook for several hours. Beer flowed generously while we waited under the moonlight, on those occasions.

Taking charge of the hotel at night had its odd responsibilities. After the office chores, I had to make sure that the help, both black and white[47], didn't make undue noises or accidentally set the hotel on fire. Mondays, being paydays for the black help, were particularly troublesome because they'd drink to excess and gamble their earnings amidst rowdy fights which I'd have to break up with the threatening baseball bat I lugged around for just such emergencies.

One evening, Harry Morel, the hotel's gay maître d', got so stoned he went to sleep with a lighted cigarette, setting his mattress on fire. Fortunately, I happened to be walking past his door on my nightly rounds when I noticed smoke coming out from under his door. Bursting in, I found Harry sound asleep on a burning mattress. I yanked him awake and tossed his burning mattress out the window. He was too far into his cups to realize what had happened, let alone thank me for saving his life.

Odd things happen in hotels at night. Once, in the middle of the night of a 4th of July Celebration, one of the College kids lit a string of firecrackers in the elevator and sent it bursting all the way to the top floor. It didn't take long for the awakened guests to light up my telephone panel, puzzling about the racket. One of those calls was more serious, however; a guest had suffered a mild heart attack, which required summoning an ambulance to take him to the local hospital. Kelly read the riot act to the student help next day, when he found out about the childish prank.

Another evening, a guest tried to reach his estranged wife in Mexico on a long distance phone call. At the time, making international phone calls on that system was a triumph. After an hour of trying, I finally connected the two of them. Trouble started when my phone panel started lighting up with several other calls and I accidentally disconnected the estranged couple's conversation. I was all apologies

---

[47] Each occupying separated basement quarters

but, like Humpty Dumpty, couldn't put them back together again after my faux pas, much as I tried. I later wondered if they ever settled their differences or went through with their threatened divorce.

I don't recall ever going to sleep on the job. At dawn, I'd sit out on the hotel's porch to watch the dolphins frolicking near the beach, that being their most playful time. One night, I saw a display of northern lights in the sky. Aurora Borealis don't usually display that far south but the strange, shimmering curtain glow couldn't have been anything else. After breakfast, I'd usually slip on my swim suit and go to the beach to sleep for a few hours under the sun, on a towel laid on the sand, soon developing a healthy tan.[48] The water in the Maryland coast was always around 55°, which wasn't conducive to long swimming spells. One night, Warren and I went skinny dipping in the beach. Overhearing our plans, some of the College girls snuck up on us and stole our clothes, forcing us to sneak back to the hotel, hiding our nudity as best we could.

Tom D'Alessandro, the then Mayor of Baltimore, owned a beach house next to the hotel. He had several children, one of whom, Nancy[49], was a friend of Robin Biddison, one of the hotel's waitresses. Robin happened to be attracted to Warren, who played her like a fiddle. Occasionally, Warren and I would double date Robin and Nancy, taking them out to some Chinese restaurant in town, catching a movie after that. I found Nancy to be a smart, vivacious 17 year-old whose quick wit and intelligent conversation made for pleasant company. I'm sure that her mother, a typical Italian mama, never quite approved of her daughter's going out with a much older foreigner. She needn't have

---

[48] which would, many years later, give my dermatologist shivers of delight with all those many basal cells.

[49] Nancy D'Alessandro, later Nancy Pelosi, would become Speaker of the House during H.W. Bush's Presidency, only three breaths away from the Presidency of the United States.

worried; Nancy and I were just good friends. In fact, she was like a kid sister to me, providing pleasant company and conversation.

There were other less intelligent College girls working at the hotel. On learning about my Spanish provenance, one of them, trying to sound knowledgeable, asked me if Prudential still owned Gibraltar. I disabused her of her notion, adding that Spanish cars had square wheels. Asked how that worked, I explained that the streets there had deep, canted grooves for the wheels to fit into. I don't think she suspected I was pulling her leg.

Ann came for a brief visit that summer. I set her up in one of the hotel's more comfortable rooms. I remember playing Beethoven's Fifth Piano Concerto over the phone for her, as a lullaby, after she'd gone to bed, while I worked at the office downstairs. I don't think she appreciated the gesture but I always loved Beethoven. I'd take her out to dinner evenings in Warren's borrowed Ford. Mornings, we'd go swimming in the beach, but it was nothing like Magalouf in Mallorca. The water was colder, for one, and there were altogether too many people around us now. I remember her getting a little uptight once when one of the young waitresses addressed me with undue familiarity. I didn't have to reassure Ann that she was, and always would be, my only true love, a feeling I truly felt all along.

The summer was over when Labor Day rolled around. All of a sudden, the beach became deserted and the hotel's help returned to their respective schools. It was time for me to start thinking about Gettysburg. I promised Kelly I'd be back the next summer, after school. Ted had arranged for me to board at the Hartzell's home on East Pennsylvania Ave., within walking distance from classes. Having offered to drive me there, Warren helped me load up my steamer trunk and leather suitcase in the back of his car and we were off on the short trip.

Chapter 10

College

"To learn gives the liveliest pleasure"

Poetics
Aristotle

One needs to have literally come off the boat to feel the wonder of America, a land the Chinese fondly call 'The Beautiful Country'. And when one does, one can think of no better greening pasture than a small liberal arts school tucked away among the peaceful Pennsylvania hills, once witness to one of history's bloodiest battles.

Miss Hartzell, my landlady of Pennsylvania Dutch extraction, was a striking, white haired lady in her early fifties who happened to be the Registrar of Gettysburg College. She lived with her 80-year old father, a retired Railroad employee who'd been gassed in the First World War. He now spent his days mostly dozing in a rocking chair downstairs, while babysitting for his grandchildren who lived next door. I was warmly welcomed to their home and assigned a sunny second floor room overlooking Highway 15. Every Sunday they'd invite me for dinner and I'd help wash and dry the dishes, for me a new American chore. Mildred was a great cook; I particularly enjoyed her rhubarb pies and apple butter dumplings.

There was a special dreamlike quality about those fall days in the Gettysburg College of 1957. The whole sniffing ritual of Fraternity Rush Week was a revelation, brothers vying against each other in bonhomie, giving sodden parties vaguely reminiscent of the San Fermin festivals. Being a veteran, I was spared the indignity of having to don the comical 'beany', making life as a freshman that much more enjoyable.

Every morning, before classes, I'd stop for coffee at the Bullet Hole, a student campus hangout. Inane tunes like "Tammy," "A White Sport Coat" and "Hound Dog" wafted out of the jukebox, mesmerizing me with their strangely haunting melodies. But it was the discovery of ham-and-cheese sandwiches and chocolate shakes for lunch at the Duncan Hines-sanctioned Lamp Post Corner, and the meatloaf and apple pie dinners at the downtown Towne Diner that convinced me I was adapting nicely to the American way of life.

But, as most fairy tales, this one, too, quickly morphed into reality once classes started, and they did so with a jolt. One of that summer's Esquire issues, which I'd read at the beach, listed several zany ways of surviving exams. Plan "A" brazenly suggested cramming one's bluebook with illegibly scribbled gibberish, arrows shooting off to the margins, pointing to highfalutin words, neatly-penned and prominently circumscribed. Equally improbable, ploy "B" proposed citing, however irrelevantly, the factoids that Michelangelo's birthday, the Turks' raid on Styria and Botticelli's painting of his *Primavera* all took place in the year 1475.

Finally, and if truly hopelessly stumped, stratagem "C" proposed turning in one's bluebook, blank save for a tearful missive to one's terminally-ill mother in Arizona, extolling the teacher's erudition and gushing on about having 'creamed' the exam. That accomplished, one dashed home, correctly filled out the exam in a spare bluebook and mailed that jewel to a puzzled mother in some fat farm out West, and then earnestly praying to God for a benefit-of-the-doubt 'D', once the mix-up had been cleared up.

The first of these artifices came in handy sooner than I expected. I forget his name now but the nice Indian professor who taught us the Contemporary Civilization course became a bosom pal overnight when, in one of his tests, I electrified him by quoting the Socratic 'know thyself' injunction in its original Greek version, Γηοθ Σέάμόη, and then going on to comment that, despite his being a stonecutter by profession, he never left us any physical trace of his work; no buildings, no sculptures, no nothing, then slipping off to preaching in the Agora. Small wonder, I conjectured, his wife, Xantipe, banished him to the doghouse! Women can sometimes be unfeeling of, and insensitive to greatness, especially if it's staring them in the face. I remember ending my criticism with: "After all, Xantipe dear, one can't be great all the time in all métiers!"

These thoughts must have touched some dim Tagore strain in my teacher's Indian soul because, flush with awe, he asked me to baby-sit for him that weekend. Not having been around babies since I myself was one, I was at a loss when the six month-old started wailing, half an hour after her parents left. A suspicious odor wafting out of the crib prompted, naturally enough, a cold, rinsing dip of the baby's bottom in the toilet bowl. The baby stared back up at me with disbelieving, saucer-sized black eyes. The procedure not only startled the child into quiescence but, in all likelihood, toilet-trained her for life.

Shainline, the Dean of Men, was next in line for my baby-sitting services. This time, however, it was I who was traumatized. No sooner had the parents left and I had seated myself on the sofa than his enormous Great Dane parked itself in front of me and rested a massive paw on my shaking knee. Baby-sitter thus immobilized and whimpering "nice dog, nice dog,", Shainline's kids had the run of the house for the rest of the evening. Large dogs and smelly diapers have remained anathema with me, ever since.

The coeval 1475 events were harder to slip in. Good old Dr. Freed, the Biblical History professor, however, made up for the shortfall with his own peculiar insistence on historical dates. The Class of '61 would, during the remainder of our College years, live in dread of encountering him on campus because of his habit of grilling us on some obscure event buried in the 5th period of Biblical History. This anxiety notwithstanding, Dr. Freed turned out to be one of my most memorable teachers. His unforgettable lectures, replete with gusts of Sinaic wind

141

and scholarly erudition, have remained with me these fifty-odd years. His learned dissertation on the JEPD[50] sources of the Torah, however, nearly got me in trouble, years later, when a clutch of earnest Jehovah's Witnesses came within an inch of collaring me with a heretic's millstone when I unwisely strewed those Freedian Biblical nuggets at them.

How forget those lengthy, after-class discussions on Biblical History with Dr. Freed. I had been intrigued by our textbook's mention of the evolution of religion from awe and wonder to ritual and dogma. To his surprise, I had connected that thought to man's need to perpetuate his beliefs in cave paintings, clay tablets or chiseled stone in order to capture his awe in petrified symbolism and thus perpetuate it. But the soul needed wings, I pursued, not trammels or congealed mementos. So, perhaps, I conjectured, it wasn't in anger but out of sheer genius that Moses broke those tablets in the Sinai. Freed appeared slightly bemused by my conclusion.

One of our most interesting discussions referred to the Patriarch, Abraham. Not having read the Bible till I took Freed's course,[51] I was surprised by the nomad from Ur's behavior, when he struck south to Egypt, keeping in the Pharaoh's good graces by allowing his fair wife, Sarah, to reside in the Egyptian's harem. Then, compounding his errant behavior, he attempted child sacrifice and evicted his concubine, Keturah, and her son, Ishmael, casting them out into the wilderness.

"Don't Muslims descend from that deportee?" I remember asking Freed. "Why do they continue to honor the Patriarch after such reprehensible behavior?"

---

[50] Jahwe, Elohim, Priestly and Deuteronomical sources

[51] Catholics were discouraged from reading the Bible's Old Testament without their Confessors' permission, probably to avoid getting children too roused by its gory, sometimes bawdy stories

I still remember Dr. Freed's limp response: "It is unfair to judge the behavior of historical characters using today's ethical standards. Odysseus would be thrown in jail today as a conniving cur instead of lauded and admired for his tricky feats."

So much for the lessons of history, I thought.

I remember being fascinated by snippets of the great Greek dramas in our Contemporary Civilization course. A particular quote from Sophocles' Oedipus at Colonus caught my attention. *"One soul can make atonement for many others, if it be sincere."* I could see in the Greek's ethereal thought – written three centuries before Christ – a definitely Christian strain, and wondered out loud to Dr. Freed how many letters St. Paul must have gotten from his Greek correspondents before writing his Letters to the Corinthians. Quoting a line from Sophocles himself, Dr. Freed shrewdly answered: "Many the wonders but nothing walks stranger than man." Talk about beautiful non-sequiturs! College professors seemed to be full of those beguiling but unenlightening witticisms.

But all were not Humanities in the Liberal Arts curriculum. There was also Physics, with the inimitable Dr. Mara, the witty, elegantly erudite Professor's Professor, who could smile even as he tiptoed through the daunting landmines of Physics. 'Charismatic' is perhaps the word that best describes someone who talked our whole Pre-Engineering class of '61 into switching to a Physics major. An inveterate pedagogue, he could not resist encouraging, cajoling, and coaxing his wards towards excellence.

One among us, John Foltz, needed little prodding, however. For four years running - and for John's benefit and bemusement - Mara would slip a tough, extra-credit question in every one of his Physics tests, bearing on some abstruse subject covered neither in his lectures nor our textbooks, simply to see if he could trip John up. He never did; John always came through with flying colors. A true individualist, John rattled the establishment in his last year of College by turning down a proffered membership to Phi Beta Kappa, not to mention a scholarship to Graduate School, though he later relented and accepted the latter[52].

Memories of College life would be insipid without flashbacks of the dull pain of exams and the unalloyed joy of half-forbidden enterprise. Jimmy Comas[53] will always loom large in my bag of College memories. Both being veterans, sharing the same major and working our way through College in the same Cafeteria, we were naturally drawn to each other by bonds of camaraderie that have defied time.

I still chuckle at the reminiscence of all those blisters he raised among the 'townies', roaring up Main Street in his infernal single-cylinder Norton motorcycle. Or the times we swiped hay from some unsuspecting farmer to use as bedding for proscribed snipe hunting parties at the historical, one-room school in the middle of the battlefield. We always kidded about our respective lab projects, he, labeling my array of cosmic ray detectors 'the greatest null experiment in Physics since Michelson and Morley's', I, baptizing him 'fly-face[54]' for the mutation-defying flies he unsuccessfully irradiated in Dr. Haskin's neutron howitzer's glory hole.

Earning our sustenance working evenings at the College Dining Hall, Jimmy and I would drive Homer, the Chef, to distraction during Friday cafeteria-style dinners, when we'd drop our ladles, stop the

---

[52] Foltz was one of three students in our class who went on to obtain a Ph.D. degree. He ended up working for the Naval Warship Center in Maryland.

[53] Jimmy was one of the three in our Class to obtain a PhD degree, becoming a research physicist at the National Institute of Standards and Technology in Maryland.

[54] one of the characters in the then-popular "Dick Tracy" comic strip.

dinner line and start soft-shoeing around him to the tune of "Jeepers, creepers, where'd you get them peepers.."

I believe it was in self-defense that Manager Overton bumped me up to head waiter at the cafeteria. When the students wearied of my same old repetitious grace over the PA system before dinner, I turned to Jimmy to spruce up my stale invocation. Picking up the mike one evening, he proceeded to perorate on the wonders of the universe and the marvel of the hydrogen atom, with its electron whirling wondrously around its proton in perfect Schroedinger reverie. I knew it was time to pull his plug when I noticed the students' bowed heads starting to bob up, trying to steal a glimpse of the deranged Strangelove at the mike.

Jimmy's divagations on the Hydrogen atom set me thinking. Never mind the story of sculpted mud origins; man was already foreordained the morning his Maker dreamt up the Hydrogen atom. But atoms by themselves, like candles under bushels, are pretty useless items. His joy of creation had to be shared with and appreciated by others, which is probably why a second and subsequent days of Creation were needed, to allow that tiny atom, His chef d'oeuvre, to evolve into sentient life. That would give Him the appreciative audience He envisioned. It would only take a second of eternity for man to know that he knew; the cathedrals and the symphonies would come soon after, as would the splitting of the atom and even lunar landings. Yes, Jimmy, that little Hydrogen atom was indeed a wondrous portent! It was comforting to know that Physics could buttress religion after all.

Three of Ann's hometown friends studying in Ivy League schools up north, stopped by to pick me up that first Christmas to drive me down with them to Chattanooga. I found Jac Chambliss the same kind, easygoing gentleman I'd met in Iloilo 12 years earlier, and more recently in San Sebastian. Bena, his wife, was equally gracious, with a more pronounced southern drawl than he. It was foggy that first evening in Lookout Mountain, where Jac and Bena lived, but they drove me around the mountain to show me the swish neighborhood they lived in.

145

Ann, who was studying for her Master's degree in Chapel Hill, turned up shortly after and it was like old times again. Her parents would discretely retire upstairs, evenings, leaving the two lovers sitting in the living room, talking and kissing till the wee hours.

The Chamblisses had a black cook, Jeanette, whose dropsied lower lip made her lisp unintelligibly. But she was a good cook. She took an instant liking to me when she convinced herself that, being Spanish, I necessarily had to be a bullfighter[55], and, hence, rich and famous. The Chamblisses also had a yardman with the peculiar name of Early Dews who, among other chores, helped shovel coal into the basement heater in winter. The emergency shelter in a corner of that basement intrigued me, the Cold War making people worry about nuclear attacks. The walled-in shelter was replete with bottles of stale water, moldy staples and rusting canned goods. It was a good thing they never had to use that shelter.

Ann's younger siblings, John and Betsy, whom I had briefly met in San Sebastian a year earlier, were working on their last years of High School, no doubt curious about the foreigner their older sister had dragged in from the cold.

That vacation, Ann and I were invited to a grand ball at the Patton's ante-bellum home in the outskirts of town. I still remember dressing up in my tux and standing in line, waiting to greet Mrs. Patton, graciously seated at the end of the third floor ball room, welcoming guests. The whole setup reminded me a little of Gone with the Wind; old traditions die hard, I supposed.

Just before New Year's, we all piled up in Jac's Delta 88 Oldsmobile and drove down to visit Bena's family in Baton Rouge, LA,

---

[55] I never even mentioned the incident at La Nouvelle Eve to her.

where her mother, brother and cousins still lived. There were few Interstate highways at the time, and not many air conditioned cars, both making for a long and tedious trip. Along the way, I remember seeing huge live oaks covered with eerie Spanish moss for the first time, figuring that's what the Deep South was supposed to look like.

My introduction to Ann's grandmother in Baton Rouge was unforgettable. On first hearing my name, "José Mari," the befuddled lady asked: "Jo-who?" and proceeded to refer to me henceforth as "that gentleman". I took the old lady's cool welcome in stride and ignored her unsubtle dig. I remember the big family dinner at some select Club where I tasted crawfish étoufée for the first time. They had good culinary taste in Baton Rouge, I concluded. We sat around the TV set in the Middleton's living room on New Year's Day, watching the exciting sudden-death play by Johnny Unitas, during the Colts' and the Giants' championship game played before New Year's.

Back in Chattanooga, I spent some time at the library doing research for a paper due in my Creative Writing course. I titled it: "Reason and Passion in French and Spanish Art," a pretty weighty subject, I recall. Flush with creativeness but pressed for time, I attributed several of my own ideas to made up sources, thus easing up on the paper's research requirements. I suppose one would, nowadays, call that "reverse plagiarism" or Wikipedia material.. Too busy sniffing out split infinitives and missing commas, Dr. Pickering, our professor, never caught on to the subterfuge.

After thanking Jac and Bena profusely for their kindness and hospitality, I took the train back to Gettysburg. It was bitter cold that winter and all I remember wearing were flimsy khaki pants and a heavy navy pea jacket. Ear muffs could have come in handy but I didn't own any.

Looking back on that freshman year, I was struck by how a fleeting gesture, a passing comment or an approving smile from one of the professors could mold one's life forever, the way a rock influences a brook's flow and direction. There was Dr. Schaeffer's Music Appreciation course, which tamed those restless souls with his Mozart arpeggios and Bach Cantatas. Equally memorable was Dr. Sloat, with his stale jokes, all lovingly annotated in his moldy notebook of Chemistry 101 lecture notes.

Physics, my major, was pretty rudimentary at first but would grow increasingly difficult in time, leaving the benumbed brain with the few joys and many scars of learning; and puzzles, too, as seemed to be the enigmatic purpose of Quantum Mechanics, or of Thermodynamics[56], for that matter. I likened them to Latin, a benighted form of mental calisthenics, devised to tease the mind and exercise its neurons. I would find out later, in Graduate School, that everything served a purpose in the grand scheme of science.

Summer break came after a grueling week of final exams. I returned to my old summer job at the Beach Plaza but it had somehow lost its sparkle. It was like Thomas Wolfe's *You Can't Go Home Again*, a second visit not quite as memorable as the first. I remember the first night at my old job; I had studied five sleepless nights in a row for my final exams and having to stay up a sixth in Ocean City, typing bills at the hotel, was taking sleeplessness a tad far. I remember falling asleep over the typewriter while typing some guest's hotel bill. Waking up minutes later I discovered that I'd typed "…psychosomatic disorders, $24" before blacking out. My last exam that morning had been in Psychology and I obviously was still divagating on the subject. The mind is a delicate machine; it doesn't take much sleep deprivation to throw it off.

---

[56] which we jokingly labeled "thermogodammits".

Warren wasn't at the Beach Plaza that second summer. I had the misfortune of having to share my room with Warren's substitute, Jack Sheridan, a football player for the University of Maryland who acted as if he'd been hit in the head once too often. He must have resented my catching up on my sleep during daytime hours, while he had to work, because he once got the lame brained idea of slipping a firecracker between my toes and lighting it, while I slept. Fortunately, the sparkling and the sizzling woke me up just before the firecracker went off. In retaliation, I lit a hammerhead[57] firecracker and dropped it in the bathroom as he was showering. Walking into the room ten minutes later, I found him in front of the mirror, making loud whistling sounds while snapping his fingers next to his ears. The hammerhead had not only broken a couple of tiles in the shower stall but must have affected his hearing as well. That was the last time Sheridan tried to wake me up.

My sophomore year in Gettysburg was almost as exciting as the first year. The weather was at its best in September and the campus was like a picture-perfect postcard. The Hartzells were their usual kind and hospitable selves. Mildred was inordinately proud every time I'd make the College's Honor Roll, proving, perhaps, that she'd made the right choice recommending me to the Scholarship Committee. I turned down repeated offers to join the Sigma Chi, Sigma Nu and Lambda Chi Fraternities because I felt it wouldn't be proper for someone on a full scholarship to spend frivolous money on Fraternity dues. Besides, being quite a bit older than any of the other members (except Comas[58]), I felt that their endless party atmosphere would interfere with my studies. Sober determination becomes an idée fixe when one starts College at the tender age of 26.

---

[57] a quarter inch stick of dynamite, whose sale was later proscribed.

[58] who, being a veteran and only four years younger than I, kept joking that 'Lacambra was really two years younger than God'.

I thoroughly enjoyed Mrs. Taylor's World Literature course, which opened completely new vistas for me. Jac Chambliss had given me a leather-bound book of blank pages which I filled with commonplace quotes and rambling comments on thoughts and subjects that appealed to me. I remember quoting those thoughts in Mrs. Taylor's blue books when comparing Don Quijote and Hamlet, Molière and Lope de Vega. She absolutely loved it and ended giving me one of the highest grades I got in College.

And, of course, there was Dr. Richardson's Philosophy course where I'd wow him with essays on Unamuno, a Basque philosopher I greatly admired. I still remember one of his quotes comparing Spanish and German philosophies:

"Light, light, I need more light" the dying Goethe is said to have cried. *"No! Warmth, warmth, I need more warmth, for we die of cold and not of darkness. It is not the night that kills but the frost. More light does not make more warmth."*

One could almost hear the Basque philosopher cry: "*I am I, but you are only you*!" "*Dar la razón*" is a propitiatory phrase seldom, if ever, expressed in a country that intuitively knows that "rightness" is neither given nor taken; it is simply possessed (by me, of course... and by Bravo).

I still remember Richardson's graceful feints to students' embarrassing queries in Philosophy class with his masterful dodge: "Hang on to that question, Miss Perisi. We'll get back to it later," a promise that would remain hanging like a lovely dangling modifier for the duration. He once suggested I switch majors from Physics to Philosophy but, much as I enjoyed Philosophy, I didn't see much future in it.

And how forget our Math teacher, Dr. Arms, who would fire differential equation thunderbolts at us, all the while trailing a peculiar

150

scent which uncharitable souls attributed to a bathtub brimming with math books.

I visited the Chamblisses again that second Christmas and enjoyed their customary warmth and hospitality. Ann was there too, on vacation from her Master's degree program at Chapel Hill, and we had a wonderful time together, renewing our troth. I remember going horseback riding with her at Reflection Riding, a beautiful arboretum on the western foothills of Lookout Mountain, which her grandparents developed and lovingly kept up. Old Mr. Chambliss once threatened to lift a Civil War tombstone now propped up in the Craven House garden, claiming it properly belonged in Reflection Riding, where the Confederate soldier had been killed.

I saw Ann again during that Spring break, having driven down to Chapel Hill with some friends of mine from Sigma Chi. I remember spending the night in their Fraternity house and coming down to my first true southern breakfast next morning, with eggs, bacon and grits, finding the latter a bit insipid. Ann was about to graduate with her Master's degree, and was writing her thesis on the subject of "Light Imagery in Shakespeare's Plays"[59].

Jac Chambliss found me a job with Combustion Engineering in New York that third summer. The Company designed and built components for utility plants, with main offices in 200 Madison Ave, a posh address. I found lodgings in a seedy boarding house in 92nd.St., corner of Broadway, run by a little old Irish lady. As expected, the

---

[59] Degree in hand, Ann later applied for a teaching job at the University of West Virginia in Morgantown, where, for the next two years, she taught a course she described as "bonehead English," mostly to football players.

lodgings weren't air conditioned. Leslie, a young Engineering student from London, also a summer hire in Combustion, shared the same boarding house with me, along with several medical students then attending nearby Columbia University.

Mornings, Leslie and I would get on a sub, get off at 34th St. and have breakfast at one of the many hole-in-the-wall short order breakfast joints, before heading for work. The first day, I noticed Leslie bristle every time one of the short-order cooks hollered: "Toasted English!" which was their shorthand for "English muffins". The second day, Leslie broke down and grumbled sotto voce: "Toasted English, toasted English! One of these days I'll order a roasted American!" I'd never seen an Englishman lose his cool since Mr. Waite, years earlier. Leslie and I became fast friends after that.

The first day at work, I was informed that my salary would be a whopping $260 a week, more than four times what I'd earned at the Beach Plaza. That pleased me enormously. I was assigned to the Company's Test Group, a small cadre of young engineers who traveled around the country checking the performance of newly designed super heater models in their newest utility plants. That implied my having to travel around the country with them and come back to analyze the data before reporting our findings.

Our first trip was to a new power plant in Anacortes, in Washington's Puget Sound, not far from Seattle. I learned all about thermocouples and heat flows and temperature gradients, and found my hands-on experience fun. Although the Seebeck Effect came in handy, Thermogodammits didn't help a bit. After work we'd stop at a local bar for beer and a game of billiards. I was surprised to discover that, in that State, one had to remain seated at the bar while drinking alcohol, nor was one allowed to carry his drink to a nearby pool table. The reason for such odd laws, I was informed, was that it was harder to pull a gun from one's holster while remaining seated. The beer's alcoholic content was a ridiculously low 1%, which no doubt also cut down on frontier brawls.

I visited Vancouver in Canada and Rockford. IL. that summer, both trips with my Test Group partners, which I got to know quite well. I remember going with them on weekend swimming parties at Jones Beach in Long Island and was surprised at the number of beer 6-packs they could put away in one sitting.

New York was hot that summer. To keep cool during weekend evenings, Leslie and I would sit through triple feature movies on 42nd. St., or catch the occasional Shakespeare play at night in the Central Park Theater. At times we'd frequent exotic Iranian, Mexican or Greek restaurants. On rare occasions, we'd order a strong cappuccino in some coffeehouse in Washington Square, where hippies tended to congregate. We once went to an off-Broadway play featuring Melina Mercouri in *Iphigenia in Aulis*, which I thoroughly enjoyed, having studied the play in Mrs. Taylor's World Lit course earlier. Life was always vibrant in New York and I could see why tourists made it their favorite destination in the US. Most street vendors, like most taxi drivers, were rude, but one learned to live with that burr.

Alfonso Bravo of Naviera Aznar had written me that spring, sending me a check for $10,000, requesting that I deposit it in a joint account with him in some Bank in Gettysburg. He explained he couldn't deposit dollars in Spanish banks at that time for fear they'd be confiscated by the *Instituto Español de Moneda Extranjera*. I was pleased and honored by his trust in my honesty and good judgment. It didn't take me long to discover the ridiculously low interest rate on Bank deposits, and suggested investing the money in the stock market, instead. With Bravo's approval, I visited a stock broker in New York that summer, who suggested investing the money in different US Utility Companies, which I did[60], quite profitably, it turned out.

---

[60] For the next two years the invested money grew to twice the original amount. Bravo later wrote informing he'd contracted cancer and would like the

Classes in my junior year started with a bang. Physics and Math courses got progressively tougher, but I always had time for my cleaner, greener world of writing. Aware of my way with words, the head of the English Dept. proposed that I be named Editor in Chief of Mercury, the College's literary magazine for that school year. The offer surprised and honored me immensely, not least because I was, after all, a foreign student. Of all the honors and awards I was to obtain later in my professional life, being the Editor of a College literary magazine as a foreign student stands out, perhaps, as my most noteworthy achievement.

Struggling all that year with a lukewarm response to repeated pleas for articles for the *Mercury*, I was delighted when an English Professor sent me a beautiful essay titled "The Hawks," supposedly written by one of his students. No sooner did that issue hit the press than the head of the English Dept. informed me that the essay was a verbatim plagiarism of one of Hemingway's short stories. My chagrin at not having recognized it in time was overshadowed by the heartbreak of learning that the student was being expelled for violating the College's Honor Code.

To fill the unforgiving gap at the *Mercury* presses, I had to resort to writing pseudonymous articles. One of these elicited an irate response from the Chairman of the Psychology Department, who took umbrage at his field's being categorized as 'a soft science'. Righteously demanding equal time, his request was gladly granted, spawning a welcome, page-filling Donnybrook.

---

money cashed and returned to him. I followed his wishes before he passed away. Too busy with school work, I later had a run-in with the IRS for having neglected to file the yearly tax returns. It took a Tax Lawyer to straighten that mess out.

Sandy Wilson, a classmate, later came to the rescue with a Salinger-type article, replete with that author's distinctive expletives. This time, hackles were raised in, of all places, the hallowed halls of the College's denominational mentors, the Missouri Synod itself. Vexed by the unsolicited and unwelcome attention from above, General Paul, the then-College president, summoned me to his office for a dressing down. Those, you see, were the fabled, no-nonsense days of signed Chapel attendance cards and proscribed panty raids.

Ann and I exchanged visits during her second year in Morgantown. During my Thanksgiving break that junior year, she came to visit me in Gettysburg, staying at the same hotel President Lincoln had slept in the night before delivering his famous Gettysburg Address. Among the many subjects we discussed during that break was marriage. She was getting antsy about having to postpone our wedding till after my graduation. After some serious, heart-to-heart talk, we decided we'd tie the knot in September of 1960, just before I began my senior year in College.

That next summer, Ann took a trip to Spain to visit Mom and, while there, order a silk wedding dress. She sailed from New York on the Monte Ulía, one of Naviera Aznar's new passenger ships plying the North American route. Being in-between assignments in New York that summer, I went to see her off.

I found one of her later stories about that trip hilarious. One evening at the dinner table, the ship's doctor overheard her crowing about playing Mus. After dinner, he arranged for her to play the Basque card game with the deck hands, in one of the ship's lower holds. In one of the game's moves, Ann wanted to bet "five more" - in Basque "amarreco" - mistakenly pronouncing it "marecón", a word dangerously close to "maricón", or "queer". The flabbergasted crewmen obviously lost that bet. After consulting his dictionary, the doctor took her aside to inform her of her faux pas. Mortified, that was the last Mus game Ann played with Basque deck hands.

She came back from her Spanish jaunt a month later, on the eve of my last trip with the test engineers to Lufkin, TX. I remember hiring Rick, a local cowhand and several of his cohorts to help handle the heavy equipment. Being the foreman of the motley crew, Rick felt he didn't have to sully his hands working, and whiled the hours away with hand motions emulating the lassoing of cattle in the range. Since Lufkin was in a dry county, Rick showed us a dive across the county line where we could have some beers after work. The place was packed with cowboys and their molls. We soon discovered that city slickers like us should refrain from ogling their girls, the cowboys being quite touchy about that. I was amused by the bumper stickers on their pick-up trucks, reading: "Built in Texas by Texans." Texans were a pretty chauvinistic bunch, I soon discovered.

Shortly after returning to New York in early September, I picked Mom up at the airport. She had come for our wedding. I hadn't seen her in 3 years but being as elegantly dressed as usual, I didn't have any difficulty recognizing her among the passengers. It was a happy reunion. I flew her down to Chattanooga to get ready for the wedding. She stayed at Ann's grandparents' house on Lookout Mountain while I stayed at the Irvin's home, one of her aunt's, nearby. Ted Ryberg, my best man, arrived shortly before the wedding. His graceful, easy-going manner, ease with words and worldly savoir faire made him fit comfortably in any distinguished crowd. I can never repay the many kindnesses he showered on me over the years.

There were parties galore that first week of September of 1960. Among them was one thrown for us by Dr. Hap Starr, Ann's old Pediatrician. Ann's grandfather, John, a card-carrying Presbyterian, was at the party. The giddy occasion made him pick up a glass of sherry from the tray being passed around by a waitress. Observing the maneuver from across the room, John's wife, the lovely Mrs. Chambliss, spoke out in a carrying voice: "John!" That's all it took for him to sheepishly put the glass back on the tray.

It was hot that summer and I spent most of my time in the Irvin's swimming pool. I was enjoying it so much one afternoon that I completely forgot I was supposed to be at my wedding rehearsal in church. Bena, my mother-in-law, frowned at my absent mindedness.

The wedding next morning at St. Peter & Paul's church downtown was impressive. The Catholic Church was packed with Ann's largely Protestant family friends. I found out later that they all tried to emulate Mom's movements in the front pew during the service, standing, kneeling or sitting as she did at the different phases of the Mass. The wedding reception that followed at Jac and Bena's home on Fairy Trail was elegant, although my best man, the ushers and I all sweltered in our winter tuxes.

After the reception, Ann and I took off in the baby blue Volkswagen beetle Jac had given us as a wedding gift. Our honeymoon's destination was the Chalet Club on Lake Lure, North Carolina. On our way there we came upon a lady in distress who'd gone off the road after her car suffered a blowout. The time I spent fixing it made us miss our first night's reservation at the Club. Hunting for a motel in Maggie Valley on our way there, we drove past one named "Teddy Bear Motel". Having voiced her disapproval, we drove on and found another one a little farther on[61].

---

[61] For years to come, I teased Ann for not remembering the name of the Motel we finally spent our wedding night in, the Skyview. To this day, she insists I suggested spending our first night at the Teddy Bear motel.

Driving up to the Chalet Club that morning the owner of the motel, who'd driven up beside us on a stop sign, rolled down his window and asked if we'd enjoyed his place the previous night. Ann restrained me from stepping out and punching him for his perceived cheek.

The Chalet Club was an attractive setting in the mountaintop across the valley from Chimney Rock, overlooking Lake Lure, NC. We booked one of the lovely outlying chalets with a fireplace, all to ourselves. We enjoyed swimming in their pool, waterskiing on the lake, playing mus[62] in the library and hobnobbing with the owners and many of the friendly guests. It was an idyllic week.

The honeymoon over, our trip up north on the Blue Ridge Parkway was memorable. We wended our way up to Frederick, Md., where we had made arrangements to rent a small apartment at the modest Stewart Manor Apartments, just 35 miles south of Gettysburg. Ann had applied for and landed a job teaching English at Hood College, a girls' school in town. We furnished the apartment with some of Ann's old furniture and acquired an old, goose-turd green sofa from Goodwill. I hooked up the new stereo system, a wedding gift from Tio José Urreaga, and played the very first tape record I bought: "Rachmaninoff on a Theme by Paganini."

Mom came to stay with us for a brief spell right after we settled

---

[62] The first argument of our married life was my disapproval of the way she shuffled the cards. Basques never shuffle the Mus cards the American way, I explained.

in, and we enjoyed her company and her cooking. I believe it was Mom who eventually taught Ann how to speak Spanish. I was, obviously, tickled at how well the two women in my life got along. Jac and Bena stopped by weeks later to pick up Mom and take her for a visit to Washington before putting her on an airplane for her return trip to Spain.

We didn't own a TV set at the time and our kind next door neighbors would invite us every Saturday evening to watch Gunsmoke episodes. Life was cozy and pleasant. I'd drive to Gettysburg every morning after breakfast to attend my senior year classes and drove back for supper every evening. Although the countryside between the two towns was pleasant and peaceful, I had to watch for deer crossing the road when it turned dark. Ann found her classes at Hood College to her liking[63]. I started putting on weight with the rich food she fixed for me and my lack of exercise. Classes that senior year were quite demanding, with challenging subjects like Classical Mechanics, Modern Physics, Quantum Mechanics and other esoteric Math and Science courses. I made sure to leave time for an elective course or two, like Logic and Dr. Sundermyer's World Literature-2, while continuing to contribute articles for the Mercury magazine, which I no longer edited.

The midterm Exams that winter were particularly harsh. I remember sweating bullets on a written, take-home exam in Quantum Mechanics. Driving to school the first day of exams, my car slid on slick ice, went over an embankment and somersaulted twice before landing upside down at the bottom of a gully. The car's battery's acid spilled all over my books and take-home exam papers but I managed to wriggle out of the wreck with no more visible damage than a bump on my forehead.

---

[63] Forewarned of Ann's recent marriage and Catholic persuasion, her boss, the Head of the English Dept., had the cheek of advising her not to become pregnant during her year's contract with the College.

I hitchhiked my way to school after the accident, arriving at a final exam in Logic half an hour late. Apprised of my accident and noticing my bruised forehead, the Professor questioned my readiness for the test. I assured him I was alright and took the exam, which turned out to be a snap. I missed only one easy question; I had to fill out the missing premise in an incomplete syllogism."Last night it snowed" read the first premise. The syllogism then jumped to its conclusion: "Therefore it's dangerous to drive today." It was the easiest question in the test but I couldn't come up with the missing premise, which was, simply: "It's dangerous to drive on snow." Forced to relive the very accident I had just experienced, my mind had simply blanked out. Despite that lacuna, I ended up with an A in that course[64].

Lacking transportation back to Frederick, I had to spend the next several nights at a friend's Lambda Chi fraternity house. When I eventually got back to Frederick several days later, I acquired a beat-up old Beetle whose dilapidated engine sounded as if it were ready to drop its womb.

I was glad when that school year was over. I had not made the School's Cum Laude roll but ended my four years with a respectable Honorable Mention. Dr. Mara, the head of our Physics Dept. suggested several Graduate School options for me, Yale, Tufts and Brown among them,, but I ended up choosing Duke University in North Carolina, mainly because of the generous scholarship offered as well as for Durham's proximity to Chattanooga.

After those four wonderful years in Gettysburg, my classmates and I scattered over the face of the land, going our separate ways, some to dream poems or minister to the sick, others to teach children or build

---

[64] A grade I always bragged about to Ann in later years, she only having obtained a B in a similar course.

things that actually worked. Some of us have, on occasion, returned on nostalgic pilgrimages to those old haunts, gratified to see the old buildings still standing, now with their pained look of age, their halls still redolent of the bittersweet smell of learning. The old professors were no longer there but their legacy remains, for much abides where, once, much was given. Gettysburg College remains a haunting place, where the love of learning still blends unobtrusively with the ghostly ancient sounds of musketry, making it a doubly hallowed place. It came as a sweet start to discover that *alma mater* stood for 'nourishing mother', for she, indeed, nurtured us well.

Combustion Engineering offered me the usual summer job with a slight salary increase, for which I was grateful. They had moved their main offices from New York City to Windsor, CN, a bucolic location near some tobacco farms. Most of the Firm's secretaries refused to move, considering Windsor a dull place compared to New York. Ann and I moved into an upstairs apartment in the nondescript town of Bloomfield, Connecticut, a few miles from work.

Besides my usual trips to inspect the Company's new utility plants, life in Bloomfield with Ann was blissful. On weekends, we'd go on picnics nearby and occasionally went to dinner and catch a movie in Hartford. We were asked to drinks with my bosses and were once invited to spend a weekend at Judy Hart's[65] parents' home near Hartford. Ann swears John, our firstborn, was conceived during that visit. I suppose women can sense such things better than men. All I remember about that visit was having an afternoon tea with the Harts' in their garden when their pooch came up from under my wicker chair and

---

[65] One of Ann's schoolmates at Connecticut College for Women.

vigorously sniffed my bottom, making me jump clear off my chair[66]. Embarrassed by my reaction, all I could come up with was the lame excuse that their dog had bitten me. Ann still laughs at the hilariously embarrassing incident.

---

[66] As they say in Spain to convince others of one's masculinity: "*Por ahí, ni el rumor del viento.*"

Chapter 11

Graduate School

"To follow knowledge like a sinking star.
beyond the utmost bound of human thought...
to strive, to seek, to find and not to yield."
Ulysses
Tennyson

We traveled down the Blue Ridge Parkway once again, this time to Durham, NC, where we found a place to rent in Poplar Apartments[67], within walking distance of Duke University's Physics Dept. It was a small apartment in a quadruplex building, with two upstairs bedrooms, a bathroom and a downstairs living/dining room area, with a small adjoining kitchen. A window air conditioner was thrown into the deal for a monthly rental fee of $90.

Our next door neighbors were the Hyatts, a Canadian couple with two kids, from London, Ontario. Jack Hyatt was working on his doctoral degree in History. Naturally enough, we soon started discussing C.P. Snow's "The Two Cultures," on the communications breakdown between scientists and humanists. The Coopers lived two apartments down, he working on his Pediatric residency. Next to them were the Grodes, a Jewish doctor from NY City married to a handsome Dominican Republic wife with swarthy features.

Around the corner from them were the Manarinos, a voluble

---

[67] Fondly known as "Fertile Acres" for the many procreating graduate school students living there.

Italian neurosurgeon married to a German pediatrician with a little girl nicknamed Shatseline. In the complex across the yard lived Mike Basset, another History Ph.D. candidate from New Zealand[68], an Egyptian couple, he an Omar Sharif look-alike studying Medicine, while next to them lived a Colombian couple, he a medical Resident, she an attractive woman from Cali who favored pink morning gowns[69], regardless of the occasion or time of day.

We'd mingle with this cosmopolitan crowd on occasional low-budget parties, money being a scarce commodity among the Fertile Acres inmates. In one of those neighborhood parties, Mrs. Hohner, wife of another History graduate student living in our complex, threw a party one evening, serving potent pre-prandial Daiquiris sans appetizers. Feeling giddy after my second brew, I fell unusually silent, snuck out the back door, staggered over to our apartment two doors down and lay flat on our bed to sleep it off. Affected the same way by her own daiquiris, the hostess also disappeared from the scene moments later. Wondering about our absence, Ann came looking for me, almost stumbling over Mrs. Hohner who was sitting on her back steps, holding her head. Ann found me, shortly after, lying on our bed, completely dressed and fast asleep.

In a neighboring building lived the Seatons, a Resident pediatrician with a lovely wife from Tennessee. They had just returned from a stint in El Paso, where he'd been serving his tour of duty in the army. While there, he'd fallen in love with Mexican culture, even joining a Bullfighting Club in neighboring Ciudad Juarez. Evenings, they'd sit on their porch, nostalgically crying over their margaritas, with soft Mariachi music playing in the background.

———————————————

[68] Later to become a member of the New Zealand Parliament.

[69] Which she referred to as her *"levantador rosa."*

Graduate school turned out to be a veritable grind. Like most graduate students, I felt I'd been ill prepared in College for Graduate School. The remedy was something called "catching up on your own." I had been granted a Fellowship sponsored by the Atomic Energy Commission, and could ill afford to relax in either my work or my studies. So it was nose to the grindstone for the duration.

I attended classes in the morning and spent afternoons in the laboratory, which boasted a Van de Graff generator that launched up to 5 MeV[70] particles. We fondly called it "the machine". We not only had to build our own electronic detectors but had to fashion our own targets and spend endless hours on the machine whenever our experiment was allotted accelerator time, sometimes for a whole week running, day and night. If I thought my night work experience at the Beach Plaza would help with my new topsy-turvy schedule, I was mistaken. Bleary eyed and unshaven, I'd take data all night and tried to make sense of my findings in the morning, after only a few winks. I envied my helpers when they walked in, bright eyed and bushy-tailed, to relieve me during the morning shift.

And how forget the infamous field days, when we had to tidy up the lab, take the accelerator apart and swab its innards with acetone. That was headache time. When we were through with the dirty work, we'd help other experimenters with their work. It was an eclectic group of young physicists, each working on their own particular nuclear experiment.

The most peculiar of the lot were two Indians who, though theoretical whizzes, were utterly hopeless with tools, not ever having

---

[70] Million Electron Volts

used one as kids. In one of my experiments, I remember having to turn the accelerator off to replace a broken target inside my target chamber. I asked Divadinam, my Indian "shifty" of the day, to turn off the vacuum pump and completely bleed off the residual vacuum from the target chamber before gently removing its top, using a screw driver in a slow, levered movement. Ignorant of residual vacuums and unfamiliar with lever actions, he tried forcing the chamber's top open before the vacuum had been totally bled, using a screw driver to forcefully push its lid up.

Unfortunately, his screw driver slipped from the lip of the chamber's lid and went straight up his nose. Responding to his unearthly shrieks, I hurriedly took the bleeding Divadinam to the neighboring Duke hospital's Emergency Room, half expecting he'd punctured his brain. Fortunately the wound was superficial and Div was back to his beloved theoretical Physics before long.

Shortly after that incident, Ann and I had Divadinam and Cyrus, the two Indian graduate students, for dinner one evening. An argument soon arose between the two about their different religious convictions. Div, a Hindu, challenged Cyrus's Christian persuasion, angels and elephants soon tussling in the fray. Ann and I found their argument hilarious, until they almost came to fisticuffs. The argument about heaven and transmigration brought back memories of my own exchange with the Buddhist monks, years earlier on the President Polk.

Classes that first year were supposed to be sedate, but they didn't quite turn out that way. I remember a particularly challenging Computer course which had us solving problems with the abstruse Machine Language's 0's and 1's. We eventually graduated to the Algol and Fortran software languages, which greatly simplified computations. There were other vaguely familiar but more complex subjects such as Advanced Quantum Mechanics, Modern Physics[71], and complex

---

[71] We had a sorry Modern Physics professor who insisted on his own misguided

Mathematics.

I purposely skipped Dr. Newson's Theoretical Nuclear Physics classes that first year, using that time more profitably working in the lab. Some older graduate student had informed me that Newson's course was a waste of time and that, furthermore, he invariably gave the same test for finals every year. Everyone has had nightmares about having to take exams in some course whose classes he'd never attended or whose text book he'd never cracked. That dreadful nightmare really happened to me with Dr. Newson's course.

A week before finals, I boned up on the questions favored in his past tests. To my chagrin, only one of his five favorite questions appeared in that year's test, this one having to do with the Nuclear Shell Model. I remember hemorrhaging over one bluebook after another on Shell Model trivia, a gusher that must have royally bored Dr. Newson to death because he mercifully gave me an "S", or satisfactory, grade for the course.

Our son, John, was born on the first day of May, 1962. I happened to be studying Hermite Polynomials when Jack, our next door neighbor, came running in to tell me that Ann, who'd been visiting with them that evening, had just broken her bag of waters. I rushed her to the Duke hospital and waited through a good part of her pre-delivery labor. Sometime during that ordeal I got hungry and, being advised that birth was not imminent, I dashed over to our nearby apartment for a quick ham and cheese sandwich. When I came back, half an hour later, the

---

approach to the subject. Years later, while working in Martin Marietta, his job application form came across my desk. I turned him down outright.

baby had been born[72]. *Qué ocurrencia*! Mom would later comment. The fact that he was a healthy boy delighted me, but when I poked my nose in the delivery room for a look at my firstborn, the obstetrician confided that the baby was too good looking to be a boy. That remark irritated me, but I said nothing. The bruises on the baby's forehead puzzled me until he explained that they were caused by the forceps delivery.

My second year of Graduate School was somewhat tougher than the first probably because I signed up for such esoteric courses as Quantum Electro Dynamics and R-Matrix Theory. Dr. Biedenharn, a noted Physics theoretician in our Department, was our teacher for the latter subject. His instructions for his course were simple: We had to attempt to solve five unsolved problems in theoretical Physics, a-la Fermat's principle in complexity, but in Physics. We'd be graded on effort. Needless to say, we spent more time trying to solve those five unsolvable problems than the course merited.

Duke always had a great basketball team. It was usually one of the top teams in the Atlantic Coast Conference Finals. Ann and I watched every Blue Devils game against their eternal rivals, the North Carolina Tar Heels. The roar in the stadium was deafening. I recognized one of those undergraduate College players in one of my graduate courses. I was amazed at how well he did scholastically, despite all the time spent practicing and playing basketball.

Our neighbor, Dr. Manuele Manarino, once asked me to accompany him on a trip to visit his friend, Monsignor Vagnozzi, the

---

[72] I'll never hear the last of that inopportune escapade for a quick bite.

Papal Nuncio in Washington[73]. We hopped into his salmon-colored Lincoln and got there late that evening. After rifling through the huge refrigerators in the Embassy's pantry, we ate a scrumptious supper by ourselves and went to sleep in fancily-appointed bedrooms.

Next morning, we had breakfast with the Nuncio and his Secretaries. After exchanging pleasantries with Manarino, the Monsignor turned to me and asked what I did in Physics. Feeling like the little boy Jesus confronted by those bearded rabbis grilling him in the temple, I told him about some pair production[74] energy calibrations I was conducting at the time. Creating something out of nothing sounded mildly heretical to Vagnozzi. Puzzled, he asked his Secretaries, sotto-voce, whether St. Thomas Aquinas had ever mentioned any such bizarre phenomenon in his *Summa*. Creation was, after all a godly attribute. I chuckled when I realized that neither the good Monsignor nor his Secretaries had apparently heard about Einstein's $E=mc^2$.

I first became intrigued with Einstein during my years in College when I came across his memorable quote:

"The most beautiful thing we can witness is the mysterious. He to whom this emotion is a stranger, who can no longer pause to wonder and stand rapt in awe, is as good as dead; his eyes are closed."

Even if the Nuncio had bought the notion of ephemeral objects, the genesis of forces holding them together would have truly floored him.

----

[73] Their friendship dated to the time Manarino assisted Vagnozzi when the Monsignor suffered a heart attack.

[74] A quaint physical phenomenon whereby a mass-less particle of light, called a photon, is transmuted into two mass-endowed particles, an electron and a positron, during its passage through an atomic nucleus.

My visit to the Nunciatura coincided with Penzias' and Wilson's discovery of an all pervading 3° Kelvin background radiation purportedly originating in the Big Bang. That was one event to make both Creationists and Evolutionists blink in wonder.

Shortly after, I learned that as early as 10^{-43} seconds after God said "Go!" the little tennis ball-sized lump of sheer energy went Bang! A mere nanosecond later, as the temperatures "cooled" down to 10^{31} degrees, this matter-shy, high energy density universe began expanding, adding space between the myriads of individual clumps of energy. As space expanded and cooled further, energy finally converted to matter. Over the intervening eons, the original "bubbles" of matter grew to become individual universes.

Cosmologists conjecture that the universe we reside in contains about 10^{11} galaxies. That's 10^{22} stars just in our neighborhood universe alone. If St. Thomas Aquinas had suspected the presence of all those many 'Earths' out there, Monsignor Vagnozzi would surely have heard about it. The good Nuncio would have drooled at the numbingly-large number of proselytes living out there, just waiting to be converted to the one true faith. Oh triple joy!

Manarino's return to Durham turned out to be eventful. Duke University had discovered that his Medical degree had been granted in Rome during the Mussolini era. Since that fascist-tainted diploma was unacceptable, he'd have to repeat his last year in Duke's Medical school and then pass the Medical Boards.

Manarino, who had been performing operations on patients' brains at Duke for several years running, was fit to be tied. Having drinks with him that evening, I noticed that his pulse trembled more than usual. I asked him how he could possibly cut into people's brains with those tremulous hands. "Oh," he responded with classical Italian nonchalance, "the human brain is a very resilient organ."

So much for delicate surgery, I concluded.

Ann and I made friends with another interesting Italian couple that summer. Dr. Ciferri, a noted biochemist from the University of Rome, had been invited by Chemstrand to come to the States and work in their labs in the Golden Triangle,[75] conducting whatever experiment struck his fancy. For some unexplained reason, he chose to study the tensile strength of chickens' tendons.

Ciferri's mind was a thing of beauty; it had the amazing capacity of using Spanish, Italian, Latin, German and French words in the same sentence, without ever pausing to choose which, always selecting each language's *mot propre* for the subject at hand. He got to calling me "*I miraggio*[76]," for always turning up at his house unexpectedly. He so loved the Blue Ridge Parkway that, while teaching his winter course in Rome and debating whether to return to the US, memories of the Parkway invariably brought him back.

I was subscribed to the international edition of Madrid's conservative ABC newspaper, to keep up with events in Spain. In one of its issues I happened to come across the verb "*esnifar*"a barbaric translation of the English "to sniff". Right there and then, I knew that the Real Academia de la Lengua Española had lost the war against Anglicism inroads.

On the first day of school, entering students in the Physics graduate program had, within two years, to be technically proficient in

---

[75] A scientific complex manned by scientists from the Universities of Duke, Chapel Hill and UNC, Raleigh.

[76] "A mirage," to which I'd respond: "*Si non e vero e ben trovato.*"

two of three foreign languages, the options being: French, German or Russian. Having passed the French test with flying colors the first day and having heard of the complexities of the Russian language, I chose German as the other of my foreign languages. I figured I had two years to learn German.

To that end, I acquired a German grammar and would open it perfunctorily every time I went to the bathroom. I started worrying when the end of the second year came around and I hadn't learned doodly in German. Working with Divadinam in the lab one evening, I learned that he had claimed English as one of his foreign languages, it not being his mother tongue. Needless to say, I followed suit.

I ambled over to the English Dept. one afternoon and, with the thickest Spanish accent I could muster, asked the Dept. Head to give me a language test in English. Suspecting a ruse, he gave me a test that turned out to be a doozy. I had to wade through endless pages of material littered with 'howevers' and "wherefore's", "nevertheless's," and "even so's" to arrive at the right answer at the end of the long article. I came out with an unheard-of perfect score, thanks no doubt to my knack in dissecting statements, honed by my Logic course in College.

The Head of the English Dept. fumed on discovering that I had obtained a higher grade than any of his English Graduate Students who'd taken that same test, an admission that pleased me enormously. "This is a farce!" he muttered, face reddening. "This is a mockery!" he added under his breath as he grudgingly gave me a passing grade in my foreign language requirement.

Dr. Ron Tilley, who guided my graduate career, was enormously helpful and generous with his time throughout my Physics career. He took me under his wing and taught me the intricacies of experimental Nuclear Physics, offering invaluable assistance throughout my career. He got me started early on a project to determine the spin and angular momenta of several lower excited states of C^{14}, using the $C^{13}(d,p-\gamma)C^{14}$ stripping reaction with deuteron bombardment of C^{13} atoms. He shared experimental time with me, substituting for me whenever I came off the machine for meals, rest, or study breaks.

It took months of accelerator time, bombarding a C^{13} foil with energetic deuterons and observing the angular correlation between the residual protons and gamma rays spewed out by the collision. The results were then analyzed and compared to the theoretical predictions in order to assign the correct spin and angular momentum of each of the lower excited states of C^{14}. My most rewarding moment was discovering a theretofore unknown gamma ray de-excitation from the third excited state of C^{14} to its ground state.

Although I finished that experiment in my third year of Graduate School, had my results published in the Physical Review publication[77] and even read a paper on the results in an American Physical Society meeting in Washington, Tilley and my other advisors considered that it was too early for me to obtain my Ph.D. degree with that experiment. Knowing that a Doctoral degree in Physics normally took five to six years, I was not altogether disappointed by their decision.

I was, at least, already halfway there. I felt sorry, however, for Ed Vizzey, a friend and companion at arms in the graduate program. He had the misfortune of choosing the doddering Dr. Hertha Sponer as his advisor in his microwave doctoral experiment. He chose her for the cachet of being the widow of Dr. James Franck, the 1925 Nobel Prize winner for Physics[78].

---

[77] Nuclear Physics, 68 (1965) p. 273

[78] Mainly for the Franck-Hertz experiment which confirmed the Bohr model of the atom, with electrons orbiting around the nucleus with specific, discrete energies.

Six months later, Vizzey showed her the first of his data from the experiment she herself had suggested. With a befuddled look, she asked: "But why are you doing this? I already did this same experiment in Göttingen in 1931!" Ed had to choose another advisor and start all over again[79]. A graduate degree in Physics can be an iffy proposition, sometimes.

But all was not work and study. Vizzey and some of his graduate school friends took up bow and arrow hunting between experiments. They'd practice shooting in back of the lab. When deer hunting season opened, Vizzey got up at the crack of dawn the first day, sprinkled some foul smelling doe scent on his hunting clothes, took off for some nearby forest and climbed a tree to wait for the first aroused buck to turn up. He never caught a deer. All he caught was the ranting of an irate wife who berated him for stinking up the house with his doe scent.

Home life in Poplar Apts. was relatively uncomplicated those days and we derived pleasure from simple things. I remember answering phone calls when Ann was out shopping, informing the caller that she was out "carousing at the A & P." We were always pinching pennies; Ann was pregnant with Laura when she once tried cutting my hair with haircutting shears I'd bought to cut John's hair, with disastrous results. The barber in town took one look at me and asked: "What happened to you?" That was the last time she tried her hand at barbering.

---

[79] Vizzey eventually obtained his degree and applied to the Navy's Nuclear Submarine School in Bainbridge, MD. He had the misfortune of working under the gruff Adm. Rickover, who refused to grant him a day off to deliver a paper on his doctoral thesis at the American Physical Society meeting in Washington D.C, only a stone's throw from Bainbridge. Years later, now a Lieutenant Commander of a nuclear "boomer" submarine, then being refurbished in Cape Canaveral, he invited Ann and me to dine with him in the impressive submarine.

Laura, our daughter, was born a year and a half after John. They didn't call it Fertile Acres for nothing, what? Born prematurely, Laura developed a respiratory distress syndrome[80] that almost did her in. Thinking she wasn't going to make it, a Coptic obstetrician in the maternity ward baptized her *in extremis*. Laura survived and has been a tough nut, ever since.

Mom came to visit us right after Laura came home from the hospital. We somehow shoehorned her into the apartment. She was not only a great help with the kids but was determined to teach Spanish to her daughter in law and grandchildren. She tried teaching little John to call her "Amachi"[81] but he only got as far as "Achi," a name she would henceforth be called by everybody.

Achi was hanging diapers in the backyard one morning alongside Mrs. Grode, the neighbor from the Dominican Republic. Having heard about our international coterie of friends at Fertile Acres and noticing Mrs. Grode's swarthy features and strange accent, she asked her if she were our Egyptian friend. That wasn't the last of Achi's faux pas. A young Japanese couple had moved into the Seaton's old apartment next door. Trying to be friendly and appear knowledgeable of their culture, she started singing the WWII Japanese war anthem: "*Komo towaku, agiano chikara, ju oku no..*" The Japanese couple was flabbergasted, militarism being a no-no in Japan after the war.

Achi used to take little John to the corner store to buy him candy. The owner's comment on John's good looks immediately put Achi on alert. She not only stopped visiting that store but started referring to the owner as "*El hombre tonto.*" She was a big help around the house,

---

[80] Also known as Hylan's membrane, a condition that had killed Kennedy's baby a month earlier.

[81] "Mother" in Basque.

175

cooking Spanish dishes and babysitting for us every other week, when Ann and I scraped up enough loose pennies to go to the movies. I remember enjoying the British spoof "Tom Jones", as well as Ingmar Bergman's "Wild Strawberries" and "A Virgin is a Sty in the Devil's eye".

Laura was a cute baby from the start. She used to give her brother John a hard time, especially while he was in the potty. I used to call her "pish-pish Bubulina", God only knows why. Even as a child she had graceful feminine movements and, when she grew enough to understand, I bet her $500 she'd grow up to be a prima ballerina in some ballet company[82].

We made the acquaintance of José María Luzón, a visiting Spanish Fulbright scholar, who used to stop by, now and then, for a hearty Spanish meal. His memory was stunning; he'd make me point at different objects around the room and assign a number to each, which I'd write down. A week later, I'd ask him to what object number 56 corresponded in the long list and he'd answer unfalteringly: "Curtain." He was, of course, right. An accomplished scholar, he went on to Germany to add another feather to his doctoral cap.[83]

Our kitchen at Poplar Apts. turned out to be a sort of neighborhood meeting ground, where we'd share our abominable home-brewed *sake* and beer with neighbors. We and the Hyatts once pooled

---

[82] Years later, she turned out to be an accomplished painter, instead,

[83] He eventually became a curator of the Itálica Museum near Seville, a professor of art history in a Madrid University and the President of the Prado Museum. We visited him for lunch on his first day at his latter job and were floored by the Goya, Velazquez and Rubens paintings hanging in his Prado office.

176

our resources to buy a washing machine which we installed in our kitchen. The tube's effluence, which normally disgorged into the kitchen sink, came loose once and spilled the dirty water onto the floor. That took a while to clean.

Our first TV set was a used, hand-me-down set from Ann's grandparents. It was a small, red colored Admiral set, with a minuscule round screen which required properly-oriented rabbit ears and a lot of imagination to view programs in the one or two channels then available. John got to see lots of underwater movies of submarines, which he called "subamarines," as well as bombers, which he called "Beftytwos." We spent one whole day watching the Kennedy assassination in that little TV set. I happened to be at the lab when it was first announced. Paul Parks, another PhD candidate with me at the time, dramatically commented: "This is going to be the Reconstruction all over again." *Exageraáo!* I commented to myself.

I was beginning my fourth year of graduate school when my team of advisers decided that I could skip my Masters degree altogether and proceed directly to work on my Ph D. thesis. Elated by their decision, I started looking for an experiment that would meet the requirements of a Doctoral thesis. I favored deuteron-stripping $(d,p\gamma)$ angular correlation experiments because of my familiarity with that experimental technique, used earlier. Half the battle in this search was identifying an uninvestigated feature of some, however obscure nucleus, capable of being excited by deuterons within the energy domain of our accelerator.

A thorough search of the existing literature revealed that Mg^{27} would be an interesting target candidate. It was known to exhibit rotational spectra associated with the shape and orientation of its nuclear field. Furthermore, it had several undefined characteristics such as the spins of its lower energy levels, their angular momentum, parity, and the multi-pole mixtures of their gamma ray transitions to ground. Determining these latter parameters would tell us something about this nucleus' sphericity, i.e. whether Mg^{27} was a prolate or an oblate spheroid; all in all, a wealth of unknowns to discover.

Although the chosen experiment was approved by my Graduate advisory board, I never stopped to consider that I'd be spending the next year adding an infinitesimal grain of knowledge to nature's inner workings. Had I been more reflective, I honestly doubt whether I'd have gone ahead and performed it. But my Ph.D. degree was riding on it, and that's all that mattered at the time.

It's interesting to conjecture how many insignificant straws of information have been added, more or less gainfully, to the Arcanum of human knowledge. I remember puzzling over the work of a coworker in Ocean City who'd spent years to obtain his Ph.D.in English investigating Ford Maddox Ford's[84] nuances of thought. But he, no doubt, thought that was an important avenue to pursue. We all have our unfathomable quirks and that's what makes us humans.

The next year was a blur of work on "the machine." One of the few happy memories I remember of those days was driving home one night after work and listening to Shubert's Impromptu in A flat Major over the car radio. I parked the car and remained there until the enthralling piece concluded and the announcer identified it. It's been one of my favorite pieces ever since.

Grode was one of the few original neighbors still hanging around Fertile Acres. I remember his complaining about his sister's not being admitted to Duke Medical School, solely because she was female.[85] I

---

[84] *Muy conocido en su casa a las horas de comer,* i.e. very well known at home at dinner time.

[85] At the time, females were non-grata Med students because of their tendency to

remember seeing the first Pink Panther movie with him. I got hooked on Sellers early on. Most of our other neighbors absconded to more fertile grounds and their replacements weren't that memorable. One of them, a hillbilly from the bootleg country of North Carolina, took his family out to visit relatives in his old haunts one day. Some bootleggers mistook them for revenuers and threatened to shoot the lot. They came back duly subdued.

Ann became pregnant for the third time around that time and Mark was born just before Christmas of 1965, a healthy, robust young boy. It was a joyous occasion and I was delighted to have a second son. I think all males have an unspoken desire to have male progeny who promise to pass the name on. That stone-aged instinct would, years later, be dubbed by feminists as "macho" or "chauvinistic".

The Vietnam War was in its first bloom, and the predictable slide into a full blown conflict irritated me. I'd have running arguments with Wiseman, a conservative graduate school acquaintance, and even wrote letters to the Editor of the local paper berating McNamara's tactics of pocking Zone D with 500-lb bomb craters or sterilizing the jungle with Agent Orange. I believe the inanity of that war was what pushed me into a Democratic political persuasion.

I finally finished my experiment and wrote up my Doctoral thesis on the $Mg^{27}(d,p\text{-}\gamma)Mg^{28}$ reaction. The day for my Comprehensive exams was set. It would be a one-day verbal exam in front of five Professors who could fire any Physics or Math question at me, on data I was supposed to have learned during my four years of College and my five years in graduate school. The one-day survive-or-perish test put the fear of the Lord in me but there was no preparation possible for that Day

---

eventually abandon their medical practice when they became pregnant, thus wasting all that valuable Med School's time and effort.

of Judgment.

As I walked out of the house after breakfast that morning, Achi promised to say a prayer for me to her little Virgin of Roncesvalles. I jokingly asked her not to call undue attention on me from above. "*Memo, mas de memo*" she answered, repeating her same response when, during the last night of the war in the San José Church of Iloilo, I warned her that all her rosary bead-clicking would give her Virgin a headache.

The Comprehensive exams were not as brutal as I expected. Only the Mathematics professor in the panel asked a question which made me hesitate. It had something to do with the curl vector representation of the force exerted on a current-carrying wire by a magnetic field, or F=I X B. The other Physics judges in the panel were as un-amused as I by the self-serving mathematician's quibble.

The end result was that I got a passing grade. It was the highest hurdle I had had to clear in nine years of almost continuous studies. I had earned the title of "Doctor," and that, of course, pleased me immensely. I don't remember how we celebrated it when I came home that evening but it must have been grand. Joy was loud and rampant at the Lacambras. To this day, I don't understand how Ann put up with so many penuries and struggles those many years. But she did, and with inordinate patience and grace. I'll always love her for it. And in that trying time, she gave me three of the finest children I could ever dream of, or ask for. Thanks for everything, sweet wife.

After later defending my thesis in front of another panel of judges, I was granted an Associate Professorship and assigned to teach Nuclear Physics to undergraduate students. I suppose the reason I didn't enjoy teaching was that I didn't have the patience for it. Furthermore, I was, burned out from all those years of almost uninterrupted studies. I needed to breathe fresh air again. I remember driving out on the Maryland countryside the day after graduating from Gettysburg College and reading Michener's Hawaii. It was a glorious, relaxing experience. I remember reading "Zorba, the Greek" in Durham, with equal feeling of release.

I could not feature myself as another Tilley, spending the rest of my life taking data points in some laboratory, guiding graduate students with their doctoral experiments. Having been there before, I was once again ready for a job in industry. With the help of some Body Shop, I started receiving invitations to different job interviews. It was the middle of February 1966 and snowing heavily in the East Coast. I remember my first job interview with Schlumberger Wells in Ridgefield, Conn. They needed a physicist to interpret neutron/carbohydrate interactions generated by small reactors piped underground in deep probes to locate new oil veins. Interesting though the job promised to be, I turned it down. There were four feet of snow on the ground in Ridgefield, and I had a miserable cold.

The next interview was with Westinghouse in Pittsburg, designing nuclear reactors. I was not enthralled with either the job prospects or the location. I was subsequently offered a job teaching at Columbia University in New York City, but I had spent enough time in that city to realize it wasn't the most attractive place to bring up a family. Finally, I was offered a job with the Aerospace Firm of Martin Marietta in Orlando, FL to head their Nuclear Effects Group. It was 83° outside when I got off the airplane in Orlando, and that alone was appealing. I knew I had found a job. The work not only promised to be exciting and reasonably well paid, but the weather was delightfully warm. Just as important, Orlando wasn't far from Ann's family in Chattanooga.

That choice made, I was required to have an American citizenship to acquire a security clearance for the job. I had longed to become an American citizen for many years now, perhaps since my years in the Philippines. With more than five years of residency in the States under my belt and being married to an American, satisfied the

181

immigration requirements. I applied for the citizenship papers at the Immigration Office in Greensboro, NC. A month later, I underwent the swearing-in ceremony and obtained my first American passport. I remember choking up while singing the Star Spangled Banner in the induction ceremony. I was now a full-fledged American and was bursting at the seams with joy.

Jac and Bena sold part of their back lot on Lookout Mountain and gave us part of the sale proceeds as a gift. With it, we acquired passage to Spain for Ann, John, Laura and me, for a two-month vacation in Spain. We decided to leave Mark, who was only 6 months old, in his grandparents' care. There was enough money left over to buy a new VW Square back in Madrid when we got there.

We took off on a flight from Miami to Madrid in late May of 1966. My job at Martin Marietta would start two months hence. It would be the first time I returned to Spain after having left it nine years earlier; I was returning with a wife, two children and a Ph.D. degree in Nuclear Physics under my belt.

Chapter 12

Return of the Native

"... How strong the pull, how clear the call,
How deep the beauty of my land, so well beloved!"

Thoughts from Africa
JML

We got on board an overnight Pan Am flight to Madrid in late May of 1966. Unable to sleep a wink, I chatted with an American entrepreneur who crowed about making a killing in Spain selling his invention of a special inner coating for sugar packets designed to keep their contents dry and fresh. I was a little humbled by the thought that he would make good with his little invention and make a better living than I would, with all my degrees. He reminded me of a millionaire biochemist we once met in Connecticut who had invented an efficient way of growing poppy seeds used for buns everywhere in the States. As a Spanish proverb states: "*A Dios rogando y con el mazo dando*[86]*."*

Luis, Maite and Achi were waiting for us at the airport. It was a touching reunion. Not having ever met Maite before, she struck me as one of those sweet, gentle souls who are, nevertheless, always in control.

---

[86] Pray to God but keep swinging your mace." I've delighted in translating that little jewel to Born Again Baptist friends who assure me salvation rests only in God's hands.

Luis chose well. Before leaving the Barajas airport, we heard a commotion outside; it was Generalissimo Franco and his aides walking up the tarmac to greet Perón himself, who had just flown in from Argentina. I remembered how Argentina used to send whale meat to Spain in her darkest, hungriest hours after the war. It tasted no different than regular steaks.

Luis, Maite and Achi were kind enough to take John and Laura with them to Bilbao while Ann and I toured Andalucía for a couple of weeks. Next morning, after taking possession of the VW square back I had ordered, Ann and I struck off to visit the sights around Madrid. Escorial was a first must stop, as was the impressive Valle de los Caídos, where Franco's remains would one day rest. We stayed at an imposing hotel on top of a hill in Escorial called, appropriately enough, Felipe II. Talking to the manager one morning, he admitted, in hushes, that he'd been a Captain in the Republican Army during the Civil War, an admission that surprised me since, in my earlier days in Spain, people had been locked up for admitting as much.

Two days later we struck out on our trip to southern Spain. Our first stop was Merida[87], where we stayed in a lovely Parador, once a convent. From there we tooled on to Rio Tinto, in Huelva, to visit José María Luzón's parents. Felipe Luzón was a Director of the Rio Tinto mines in the outskirts of town, an impressive cavity in the earth, dug out originally by the Romans to extract copper and sulfur. The mines provided work for most of the town folks. The Luzóns proudly showed us the small museum built by their son, José María, to house Roman tombstones, coins, oil lamps and other artifacts he'd discovered around the mine, as a teen ager. Small wonder he grew up to be an Archeologist

---

[87] A city in the province of Badajoz in southwestern Spain, named after Emerita Augusta, one of Augustus' Legions stationed there around 25 AD to defend Rome's westernmost province of Lusitania.

of note! Being a good cook, Mrs. Luzón prepared some great gazpacho for us, an Andalucian soup most northern Spaniards frown upon, not knowing what they were missing.

Mr. Luzón drove us around to visit several sleepy towns in the area. I still remember the little hermitage on top of a hill named Nuestra Señora de Los Angeles, after whom the city of LA in California was named by a local Conquistador. Mr. Luzón then drove us to Cortés' castle and the ruins of other palaces nearby, once belonging to his lieutenants who, having once been pig herders, made good in the "Indies". We stopped in another sleepy little town to buy a Jabugo[88] ham for Luis and Maite in Bilbao.

Our next stop was the fancy Hotel Alfonso XIII in Sevilla. Not having made reservations, we were assigned a tiny room in an unbearable hot attic. Mrs. Luzón guided us up the Giralda tower and Parque Maria Luisa. We toured the caves of Sacromonte one evening and were treated to flamenco dancing. Like gazpacho, gypsy flamenco dancing was looked upon with disfavor by the snobby Basques.

Following José María Luzón's suggestions, our next stop was the Parador in Arcos de la Frontera, near Jerez. It wasn't open to the public yet so we proceeded on to Ronda. The dark, winding road along the side of steep cliffs was scary. Because my headlights were stuck on high beam, I had to stop and turn my headlights off whenever oncoming traffic drove past. Ronda was well worth the effort. We stayed at the Palace Hotel which overlooked an impressive gorge. Breakfast in bed with fresh Spanish orange juice was the *ne plus ultra*. The town, with its winding streets and overhanging bridges, reeked of age. I'd never seen anything as dramatic.

---

[88] Acorn-eating pigs producing expensive hams now called jamón Ibérico, pata-negra or simply jamón de Jabugo..

The pièce de résistance of that southern excursion was Granada, the last Moorish stronghold to fall to King Ferdinand and Isabel's armies the same year America was discovered. We were lucky to stay in the Parador San Francisco, smack in the heart of the Alhambra. The exquisite workmanship of Moorish filigrees in every corner of the enclave was breath taking. It comes as no surprise that when he saw a blind child begging in Granada, King Ferdinand asked his wife:

"Dale limosna, Señora, porque no hay nada más triste que ser ciego en Granada.[89]*"*

Anything after that display of Moorish beauty was bound to be anticlimactic. Even our next stop, the Parador of Jaen, a stunning medieval castle set in the middle of olive groves, was a downer. Toledo, perhaps, was a passable second best. We drove by there but not having Arturo's address with me, we moved on.

We'd been away from the children for several weeks and getting back with them in Bilbao was sheer delight. John, who was four years old then, found Bilbao "polluted," just as his father had, 17 years earlier. He didn't make any bones about it, either, and told Maite so. She was surprised and not a little shocked at this young American's sagacity and forthrightness. The Altos Hornos and La Naval were still going strong and their combined emanations were as suffocating as I remembered them nine years earlier. Our kids enjoyed playing with their cousins, who were their age. Their governess would take them for walks to Plaza Elíptica, where they'd gorge themselves on *cacahuetes* peanuts and rolled *barqui* cones.

Achi was living with Luis' family. He had moved from Aznar and now worked for Artola, another local Shipping Firm. He had found

---

[89] Give him alms, milady, for there's nothing sadder than being blind in Granada.

his ship brokerage groove. After a few days with them, I felt like visiting the prehistoric cave paintings of Altamira, west of Santander, in northern Spain and, and, if possible, the historic cave of Covadonga a little farther west. Since Luis was on a business trip those days, his wife Maite decided to travel with Ann and me.

We stopped at the little fishing village of Noja, near Santander, picked out our own lobsters from their sea pens and had a delicious lunch. We then proceeded to Altamira. The caves and their paintings were impressive, particularly those along the walls of a confined circular space with a passageway around a large boulder. It wasn't long after our visit there that the Ministry of Archeology stopped tourists from visiting the cave altogether. The bacteria in human breath were causing fungus to grow and deteriorate the 15,000-year old paintings. They now have a replica nearby, for tourists, but it's not the same.

We had to skip the quaint Parador de Gil Blas in Santillana del Mar, near Altamira, because Maite prudishly refused to sleep in our bedroom's adjoining alcove, so we drove on to Ribadesella, a coastal Asturian town, where we found rooms in an old Marchioness' mansion. The reflections from the bathroom's completely mirrored walls and ceiling were startlingly revealing. I conjectured that the Marchioness must have been young and in good shape.

From there, we drove on to the caves of Covadonga on the side of a high mountain. Inside, was a large church with daily services to commemorate the Christians' victory against the Moors, the first of many in Spain's centuries-long struggle to regain their country from the North Africans. It was interesting that, in the span of less than a month, we had visited what took eight centuries to accomplish; the beginning of the resistance in Covadonga and the final Christian victory in the Alhambra. Talk about inhaling history!

We drove back to Bilbao to pick up Achi and the children and headed for Burguete. The Loizu was the same old quaint, comfortable hotel and I was proud to show off my progeny to their Navarran great grandmother, their aunts, uncles and cousins. Little John was particularly impressed by the minnows swimming in the Urrobi stream, which he fancied to be "whales," and tried unsuccessfully to fish. The kids, like their father, enjoyed fried eggs and *longaniza* for breakfast, as well as the wild strawberry-laden thick yellow cream for dessert. They were awed by farm life, in particularly the huge pigs in the basement's sty, the warm milk Alberto squirted on Laura's face while milking cows in the morning, the San Juan festival in late June, with all its bonfires and noisy merrymaking.

Alberto was not too impressed by my degrees or years of studies. To cut me down to size, he handed me a scythe one day and asked me to help him and some hired hands to manually mow hay and then haul it up to the house's attic for the cows' winter feed. It was back-breaking work. He sniggered when he saw me breathing hard, taking breaks and nursing blisters, and mocked my suggestion that they acquire a tractor. Mountain folks are generally suspicious of city slickers, especially those with advanced degrees, and loved to show them up on every occasion they could. They even coined the name *"indianos"* for immigrants returning from years of hard work from the Americas[90].One of these well-off immigrants once returned to Burguete with a Buick, which he pronounced "Booick," a moniker he'd carry till he died; even his sons and grandsons would forever after be known as the son, or grandson of "the Booick." Mountain folks are merciless; perhaps that's why they

survived the millennia.

Ann and I drove back to Bilbao to attend Vicky Urreaga's wedding. Tio José and tía Mariví were their usual charming selves. Mariví, my old, frustrated flame, eyed Ann

---

[90] Which Columbus erroneously called the "Indies."

suspiciously, thinking, perhaps, that that could be she. Julio Múgica offered to transport my new VW back to the States in one of the Aznar ships for free, an offer I couldn't refuse. I would pick it up in New Orleans a month later[91].

After saying our goodbyes to the family in Burguete, we took the train to Madrid where we boarded a plane back to the States. It had been a glorious vacation which we would never forget. Our TWA flight back was cancelled at the last minute for mechanical problems. We were then slapped into First Class in a flight to New York, via Copenhagen, where we spent the night and next morning visiting the Danish countryside. On the trip back to the States, out tickets were, once again, upgraded to First Class. Travelling with a good looking wife and young children had its advantages those days.

We eventually flew into Chattanooga, where we saw the Chamblisses and, of course, our now 6-month old son Mark whom they had babysat for two months. The happy, bright-eyed kid didn't look the worse for wear. Hopping on our Comet station wagon we drove to Orlando the last week of July, arriving in the middle of a torrential downpour. We would get used to these tropical, one-hour phenomena in summers to come.

---

[91] without any nicks or dents

Chapter 13

Orlando

'Thou shalt not be afraid for any terror by night;
nor for the arrow that flieth by day.'

Psalms 17

We spent the first few days looking for a place to rent in Orlando, preferably near work. We found a nice little house on Glasgow Ave., by Lake Cane, near where Universal would eventually build its entertainment complex. There were several small lakes in the neighborhood where I went fishing the first afternoon. A large, aggressive largemouth bass swimming in the shallows turned around and bit the tip of the fishing rod with which I was prodding it. That was sobering. Another afternoon, walking in a sandy path amidst Florida brush near home, I was startled by a large reddish-gray Florida Panther that crossed my path in a blur. Wildlife in Florida was more interesting than I had anticipated.

My first day at work was exciting. After being interviewed by the Systems Manager to whom I was to report, I was put in charge of the Nuclear Effects group, manned by about a dozen employees versed in Physics and Computer science. It was at the height of the Cold War, when Russian intercontinental ballistic missiles threatened to annihilate the U.S., and vice versa. The schizophrenic game of tit-for-tat was labeled, appropriately enough, MAD, an acronym for Mutual Assured Destruction. It was a bizarre new world I'd stumbled into and its very un-realness made it weirdly exciting.

Most of our programs operated under the auspices of the U.S. Defense Department. Martin Marietta had been contracted to develop the Sprint missile, a, fast, last ditch defense missile designed to intercept Soviet Intercontinental Ballistic Missiles that leaked through an exoatmospheric defense shield. And it had to do it in no more than a couple of heartbeats. Practically every subsystem of the Sprint missile pushed the envelope of the technological state-of-the-art, from its guidance, to its aerodynamics, to its control and propulsion systems. It was a thing of breathtaking complexity, almost every technology in it unproven and untested. And there was a lot of pressure from above to make it work. And quickly!

Since the missile was guided to its target by a relatively inaccurate ground based radar, the miss distances achievable against a threat missile were too large to destroy it with anything but a low-yield defensive nuclear weapon. Even so, Sprint's on-board nuclear device had to be detonated at the right time and in the close vicinity of the incoming nuclear weapon in order to neutralize it.

At the time, the required lethal miss distance was speculative. And that's where a nuclear physicist came into the picture. I not only had to figure out the maximum miss distance allowable for the radiation level from our device to melt the incoming warhead but achieve it within the guidance and aerodynamic constraints of our defense missile. It was a tall order that required close cooperation and constant consultation with scientists in the National Laboratories who built and provided the nuclear device.

I had to quickly acquire familiarity not only with the radiation spectrum emanating from our weapon itself but develop complex computer programs to determine the propagation and attenuation of its various radiations through space.

It took my computer experts several months of intricate computations to establish these lethality characteristics. And computer computations did not come cheap those days. I remember submitting huge decks of punched cards to the Company's main computer for overnight computations. Our Department Head croaked every time he got the bill for those computations. There were also trips to several Government nuclear Laboratories like Los Alamos, Livermore and Oak Ridge, as well as visits to other defense Firms to share our findings and corroborate our results.

The Defense Dept. required regular reports and presentations at different locations in the country, which meant I had to prepare and write voluminous reports, and travel frequently. I was living in a dark, mysterious world, where I couldn't reveal even the nature of my work to anyone except those with whom I worked. It was a hectic, secretive, tantalizingly complex job.

I didn't have trouble compartmentalizing my life, however, keeping my work separate from my cleaner, greener world. My work grew so sensitive that it didn't take long before I required a Top Secret clearance and other, even more restrictive clearances. Drugs, excessive alcohol indulgence or illicit sexual activity were as taboo to the Intelligence folks as being a homosexual or belonging to the Communist party. One needed a clean record for those clearances. I remember some snoop from the National Intelligence Service stopping by my office one day to ask probing security questions of my life. He chuckled when I confessed to having once smoked a weed when I was in the Spanish Army, and paying for it dearly with a doozy of a headache.

I remember working with a Jewish co-worker on a new Nuclear Effects contract in 1967. It was the year when the 6-day Israeli/Arab League war erupted. He went on about the Israeli victory over the Arab League. I simply kept my peace. Goldmacher got so excited he developed ileitis, an intestinal disorder that cost him a large segment of his small intestines.

That was also the year my son John turned five. The children were growing up and I tried to be friendlier and much more accessible to them than my father had been with me. On his birthday, I took him and five of his neighborhood friends to Gatorland as a birthday treat. We watched one of the rattlers in a snake pit slowly climbing up a tree, slithering along an extended branch and dropping beyond its confining enclosure, right at the feet of a black woman who happened to be walking by. Turning almost white and shrieking hysterically, she ran away from the snake and into a herd of aggressive geese, which proceeded to noisily attack her. It just wasn't her day. John and his friends giggled at the commotion.

It was already six o'clock and all the other tourists had left. As a grande finale of the birthday treat, I led the five kids to a cage holding a giant white python. Unbeknownst to me, it was the snake's feeding time and the keepers had just snuck a little white rabbit into the snake's cage for its weekly feeding. Unaware of its impending demise, the rabbit pranced about happily around the cage. The python hungrily eyed its prey, following its every move with a flicking tongue. Then, quick as lightning, the python struck, coiled itself twice around its prey and strangled it. It was a gory spectacle: eyes popping out of the rabbit's orbits, blood oozing out of its mouth. Hard as I tried to pull the kids away from the gruesome spectacle, they remained glued to the glass, utterly mesmerized. I caught hell from the mothers of every one of those kids for their recurring nightmares the nights that followed.

The Anti Ballistic Missile treaty signed between the United States and the Soviet Union came into effect just after our Sprint missile had been tested, proven effective and fielded. It hurt to read that concrete had been poured in the silos built to house the missiles we had spent so many man-hours developing and testing.

194

Strange to say, that Treaty didn't stop the government's ABM technology investigations. Much remained to be learned about whole new concepts of ballistic missile defense. I headed several studies aimed at developing more modern and survivable defense systems. Under the Company-funded internal research and development (IR&D) efforts, I came up with a self-contained ICBM defense system consisting of an air cushion vehicle equipped with an onboard radar and a complement of small Sprint-like defense missiles. The idea was to scoot around the Minuteman silos and defend them individually, relying on the ACV's mobility for survival. Although the novel concept earned me the Company's yearly Meritorious Award, the tank-bound mentality of Army Generals didn't quite buy the concept[92].

I later directed a major study titled "BMD of the Nineties," a futuristic, far-out defense system to counter Soviet threats of the future. It gave me great pleasure to snag the Boeing Company to partner with us in that effort. It turned out that the favored defense construct we came up with was outrageously expensive and I admitted as much in my final presentation, to the consternation of the BMD community's fat cats sitting in the audience. My last summary chart quoted several classical Greek heroes to make my point. Mention of Procrustus[93] started the shock wave rolling when I blamed the ABM community of purposely making the threat worse than it was. Gordius[94] followed with the brute

---

[92] The soberside Admirals and Generals calling the shots before the Second World War also ridiculed Billy Mitchell's third-dimensional air warfare when he first proposed it. The Pearl Harbor disaster proved them tragically mistaken.

[93] A rogue smith and bandit of Attica who attacked people, stretched them or lopped off their legs to make them fit his bed's size. A Procrustean approach fits a threat to an arbitrary standard.

[94] The legend of Gordium claimed that he who unraveled the difficult knot would be the master of Asia. Alexander took one look at the complicated knot and simply sliced it in half with his sword.

force approach to solve an unsolvable problem. Quoting Midas suggested that only he could afford to pay for the system's outrageous cost. I now forget who the fourth mythological character I quoted was but the whole idea of bringing candid thought to a knotty problem was a revelation to that inbred community. Back at the office, my Presentations crew was surprised and delighted by the history lesson approach and chuckled over the *cojones* it took to present that summary viewgraph. Although the powers that be in the BMD community commended my performance, my Billy Mitchell approach was not altogether palatable to some.

We made it a point to go to Spain on vacation every other year, to touch bases with the family. As the children grew up, they'd interchange summer-long visits with their Spanish cousins, who now lived in Madrid and summered in El Escorial, Luis' girls coming to the States during one summer to learn English, our kids spending the next summer in Spain to improve their knowledge of Spanish. Of our three children, Laura got the most out of those interchanges, mainly because she had cousins her age there. She picked up a perfect Castilian accent, as she later did French[95]. The boys also picked up some Spanish but, not having male cousins their age, their Spanish always had a slight American trace.

Ann was getting tired of having to drive long distances to do the shopping. Besides we were ready to buy, rather than rent a home. We

---

[95] Both of which would come in handy, years later, when she worked for Disney World's Guest Relations, and got to guide such important guests as Don Juan, King manqué of Spain, the Presidents of France, Norway and Paraguay, and even the CEO of Sony Corporation, who took a shine to her and insisted on giving her expensive gifts which she couldn't accept..

eventually moved to a nice Georgian house built in 1937, under a canopy of oak trees overlooking Lake Virginia in Winter Park, right across from Rollins College. It meant a longer drive to work for me but the new location was well worth it. We quickly made friends with our neighbors and I got to play tennis practically every Saturday morning with Jack Lane, a next door neighbor, Professor of History at Rollins College. I remember playing five sets in the heat of the noonday sun[96] and then mowing our yard to top off the Saturday activities. Ah youth!

The kids started attending Mrs. Achenback's elementary school[97], moving after their third year there to Parochial schools, first at St. James then later to St Margaret Mary's. Laura and Mark both had a knack for art and took art lessons at a local Art school in town. Asked to draw a house at the tender age of three, Mark invariably drew it from an isometric projection, as if seen from an angle from above. His sense of space was uncanny, Escher-like. John, meanwhile, got in trouble with his coach at St. James, who claimed he called him a name. John, to this day, assures me he only called him "sheep head". He had a crush on someone called Melody Zeitung, a name which no doubt destined her to a life of belly dancing.

Ann was always looking for the best school for our brood. When they were old enough, she decided to enroll them in Trinity Preparatory School, one of the best in town. The expensive tuition made her consider teaching English there to defray the cost. Little did she know when she applied that the only opening being offered that year was to teach Latin. Having taken seven years of that language in High School and College, she decided to take the job anyway.

---

[96] Mad dogs and Englishmen and crazy Basques, out in the noonday sun.

[97] A tough school teacher of German extraction, who, I always suspected, prompted her class to say "Sieg Heil!" in lieu of pledging allegiance to the flag.

It was not easy for her at first but she soon grew into the job and became an excellent Latin teacher. She had those kids under control from day one. It's not hard to see why. Proof of her knack for teaching was that her Latin students always won top honors in all the State *Certamens* they participated in. It was a little awkward at first for our kids, having their mother as their Latin teacher. Indeed, in one of her classes, Mark was heard to grumble out loud: "But Mom!" complaining about some tough homework assignment she had assigned the class. But they survived each other. She was soon named head of the Foreign Language Dept., in charge of the Latin, Spanish and French teachers.

The boys were fortunate to attend a Prep School where they could play junior and varsity basketball early on. Mark later also picked up football, a sport that worried his mother, especially when she saw an ambulance parked alongside the field's sideline before every game.

One night, Mark and some of his football teammates decided to play a prank on David Lilly, their team's quarterback. Taking my sunfish sailboat out on Lake Virginia, armed with a powerful flashlight and a roll of duct tape, they snared a young two foot alligator attracted by their light, hauled it in, taped its snout with duct tape and took that jewel over to Lilly's home. They somehow snuck into his room, lifted the bed sheet covering their sleeping friend and slipped the live alligator next to him. The reptile's violent movements woke Lilly up, scaring him half to death. After they had had their laughs, they took the alligator, unwound the tape from its snout and threw it into the Lilly's swimming pool. Everything calmed down until next morning, when Mrs. Lilly jumped into the pool for a morning swim to find an alligator swimming alongside her. After the Fish & Game Commission folks retrieved the reptile, Mrs. Lilly took David's teammates to task.

Of all our three kids, Mark always seemed to be the most adventurous. His head would have been a phrenologist's delight from all the knuckle raps he got over his growing up years; there were no "time-outs" then, you see. I remember buying a new Honda Accord Hatchback and forbidding anyone in the family from even touching it. Mark, then 13, picked up my car keys one night, jumped out his bedroom window to the garden below, got in the car and drove off to pick up his buddy, Frank Weber, for a midnight joy ride. While driving through Winter Park, they were stopped by two patrolling policemen, who shone their flashlights at them. Obviously looking for a specific criminal, they let them go without realizing the two kids were way under their lawful driving age.

Achi came to visit us every other year, and would stay for as long as half a year with us. She was great company and everybody loved her. To this day, friends will refer to Achi as a lovely, elegant lady. She was intelligent, well read and had a ton of savoir faire with which she could mesmerize a stone. On one of her trips, she brought her sister Beatriz along and we had a wonderful time together. Tia Beatriz, a retired school teacher in San Sebastian, loved to walk. She struck off one morning, not knowing either a word of English or exactly where she was going. She promptly got lost and Ann struck out in search of her. She was eventually retrieved and her sister Achi admonished her, murmuring: *"No se te caerá la casa encima, no!"*[98]

My first cousin Quiquito , whom I first met in Pamplona and who'd been slapped into a Capuchin monastery for failing math in High School, was eventually ordained a monk. Fancying missionary work, he was sent to proselytize native Indians in the highlands of Ecuador. He came to visit us in Winter Park on his second sabbatical leave and had some funny stories to tell.

Quiquito appeared subdued and uncharacteristically introverted when we first saw him. He had lost some of his old spunk, a condition

---

[98] "The house won't ever fall on your head, will it?" chiding her for always being out and about.

he himself attributed to his mind's being touched by "a little jungle rot" after all those years in the wilderness. His life in the Ecuadorian jungles appeared to have taken its toll. His greatest regret, he admitted, was not having been able to properly proselytize his Indian wards during his long stay with them, their religion now an ungodly mélange of superstition and Christianity

His mission among a tribe of Ecuadorian Indians happened to border a mountain brook across which lived a tribe of honest-to-goodness headhunters, with whom his people were constantly skirmishing. Quiquito prayed for the chance to learn the headhunters' dialect so he could one day come close enough to proselytize them. His prayers were answered one night when one of the attacking headhunters was wounded on his side of the brook and was taken captive by his people. Quiquito took him to his infirmary and slowly nursed him back to health, all the while attempting to learn his patient's dialect.

Halfway through this learning process, a group of American Baptist missionaries who happened to be camping nearby had apparently heard, through the vine, about this wounded headhunter's whereabouts. Believing they had as much right to learn his dialect as the Catholic missionary next door, they slipped into his infirmary one night and absconded with his prisoner. Quiquito was fit to be tied. Needless to say, Baptists have become anathema to him up to this day.

During his stay with us, Quiquito slowly groped back to his normal self. He even ambled over to our parish church every morning, asking if he could celebrate Mass. Not having learned any English, he tried communicating with the Irish pastor in Latin, a reasonable but fruitless try. He was nonetheless lent a large surplice and chasuble with which he celebrated Mass in Latin, greatly mystifying the few stragglers attending the service.

One morning he asked Ann if he could borrow her car to take a spin around town. He struck off undeterred and soon found himself tooling down I-4 in Ann's "green bomber", as the kids called her derelict Buick. He soon noticed smoke billowing out from under the hood and decided to pull over. Noticing his predicament and distressed look, a kindly State trooper pulled over to help. To his English query, the distraught monk could only respond: "No speech English. *Telefón! Telefón!*" The trooper asked Quiquito to hop into his cruiser, offering to take him to the nearest gas station to make a phone call. Observing Quiquito fumbling with his Ecuadorian coins, the trooper gave him a dime to make the distress call. When he finally got through to Ann, all he could mutter was: "*Oye Ana, estoy en un apuro!*"[99]

Quiquito's brief vacation in the States soon came to an end. We saw him off at the airport and never heard from him again until someone in the family told us he had "hung up his robes," a quaint way of saying he had left the Order of Capuchin monks and was back in the world of the living, as a layman. We learned that he was making a living teaching Electronics (!) at one of the Universities in Madrid and that, *mirabile visu!* had even married and was bringing up a family

But that was not the last I'd hear from Quiquito. One day, waiting for our plane at the Barajas Airport in Madrid, who would turn up but Quiquito himself. He was smartly attired and slightly more mature than his graying sideburns betrayed, but his crinkly eyes still revealed the old impish look. He had stopped teaching Electronics at the University, he admitted, because the pay was not good enough to bring up a family properly. So he had slugged through five years of night school to become a Lawyer! Now, he said, he was an Advocate of some renown in town.

One summer our family joined my in-laws on a trip to England. We concentrated on London and the Cotswold's on that trip. We had a

---

[99] "Hey Ann, I'm in a bind."

wonderful time visiting several grand English Manors. One day, lost in a round-about looking for Studley Priory, our next manor house stop, we noticed a Bobby watching us going round and round in endless circles. Hopping on his bicycle, he rode up to give us directions. On our way back to London three days later, we found ourselves lost in the same round-about, looking for the nonexistent exit to London. The very same Bobby turned up, approached the car once again and asked in a lilting voice and a delightfully wry British humor: "Still looking for Studley?"

Ann used to watch John like a hawk during his teen years. One evening, she discovered that he wasn't home where he was supposed to be, doing his homework. Smelling a rat, she called our neighbor Mrs. Baldwin to see if John were playing Dungeons and Dragons with her son, John. Apprised that they'd gone to the movies instead, she dragged me along in search of John. We eventually found him and John paid dearly for his escapade.

I was 44 when I suffered a minor heart attack. I'd been eating too much cholesterol-rich food and smoking heavily while working hard at a special project at work. After being released from a short, two-day stay at the Florida Hospital for observation, I took a week off from work and took Ann and John to Abaco Island in the Bahamas for a restful vacation. Our Motel was by a beautiful lagoon where John and I went snorkeling every morning. One day we swam directly over a largish shark just resting there, at the bottom of the ten-foot deep lagoon. We made haste swimming back to the beach. As we sat there mulling over the shark, I told John that it was probably a hoax to scare tourists away. I knew sharks had to keep moving to keep alive, and that one was certainly not moving. To my suggestion of going back and poking the fake shark, John responded: "You go!" That was a smart answer because after later turning in our snorkels we were informed that it was a live nurse shark, one of the few species that can breathe without moving.

The year came when John graduated from Trinity and went to Emory University in Atlanta as a Merit Scholar, taking his skate board for transportation around campus. He had spent a summer with Outward Bound in North Carolina which, no doubt, toughened him up. To make money that following summer, he sold books in Kentucky for the Southern Book Company, riding a clunker without a reverse gear, which made him avoid parking in dead-end alleys. He admitted that his prize feat was selling High School textbooks to a recently married woman who wasn't even a mother yet.

John started out as a Psychology major but in his junior year of College I talked him into switching to Medicine, which he did. He later attended South Florida Med School and took his ER residency in Toledo, OH to finally practice in Seattle, WA.

 Mark got accepted to the School of Architecture in the University of Virginia. His natural artistic talents made that decision a no-brainer. On his graduation day, one of his classmates confessed that Mark was the most talented student of his Architecture class and that he'd one day end up being a famous architect. Mark was hired by an Architectural Firm in Richmond, VA, shortly after, but disliked the "gopher" work so much he resigned and worked in Washington DC for a while, remodeling homes in the winter and then reverting to his summer job in Maine, as counselor in Outward Bound. There, he met his future wife, Deirdre, also a counselor at the same camp[100]. After a while, Mark decided to go into medicine and, after eight more years of study, became a physician specializing in Family Practice. I don't think he was consciously trying to emulate his father's endless years in school. John met Rebecca, one of Deirdre's old

---

[100] Years later he single-handedly added a second floor to his fairy tale house, and later built a nice log cabin in the Washington wilderness, also single-handedly.

classmates, at Mark's wedding, and married her shortly after. Both brothers, now Physicians, live in Seattle

Laura chose to go to SMU College in Dallas, where she majored in Fine Arts. She spent her junior year in Paris, studying art while boarding in a house on Île de la Cité, right across from Notre Dame. Being a natural for languages, her French, like her Spanish, was perfect. Her year in Paris allowed her to hone her artistic talents to the point where she would, years later, become an artist of note.

My heavy smoking took its toll. In 1979, at age 48, I underwent open heart surgery for two coronary bypasses. I timed the operation a month before Luis, Maite and their son Javier came to visit, so that I could play tennis with my brother during his stay here. During his visit, Javier suffered a diabetic coma, a condition that would stay with him during his brief life. A year later, Mark and I laid down an irrigation system in our yard. I remember manhandling the heavy trencher, just to prove I was back in shape.

I believe it was 1983 when President Reagan got the ABM community up on an excited state with his Strategic Defense Initiatives speech. He had had enough of the Cold War psychosis and decided to shake the Soviets out of their snug MAD mentality. To that end he injected a renewed impetus into the then anemic Ballistic Missile Defense effort. A defense shield would be built and deployed to blunt the Soviet ICBM threat with powerful exoatmospheric and endoatmospheric layers. The former would be equipped with potent geo-stationary lasers as well as a galaxy of miniature kill vehicles launched from earth-orbiting space-based mother ships to intercept the ICBMs before they could deploy their multiple reentry vehicles and decoys. The lower, or endoatmospheric layer, would consist of advanced land based missiles that would intercept any RVs leaking from the upper defense tier.

Our Company's Denver operation would handle the exo defense system while our Orlando group would design the endo defense system. Having been steeped in just that kind of work for years, I was designated technical director of the SDI's endoatmospheric system proposal to the Army. Six months later, our final presentation to Lt. General Abrahamson, in charge of SDI in Washington, took one whole day and was well received. The General even sent our Company President kudos for my personal contribution to the study, complete with a happy face by his signature. We, along with McDonald Douglas, one of several competing teams, ended up winning contracts to compete for building and deploying the system.

The system was so thoroughly awesome and credible that the Soviets blinked. SDI was later purported to have caused the eventual demise of the Soviet Union. Reagan took credit for the feat but he was well backed by an army of dedicated scientists. The Press, which had dismissively referred to SDI as "Star Wars" all along, was duly subdued. I can claim a small feather in my cap for that development.

A summer later, I decided to take the two boys backpacking in the Appalachian Trail. We spent a wonderful week trudging up and down the Smoky Mountains, eating freeze-dried food and sleeping in bear-proof shelters. John shooed a female black bear and her two cubs away from the shelter the afternoon we got to Spence Field, in whose shelter we had reserved "lodgings."

We spent the last night of that trip, on Mount LeConte, near Gatlinburg, where we had usurped three bunks in a shelter the night before we were supposed to arrive there. Two drunken backpackers turned up at midnight and, seeing their bunks taken, pitched a tent outside the shelter. At about four o'clock that morning, I felt an urge to relieve myself just as a bear came up to the shelter's door and banged on it, trying to get at the food it smelled inside. I never knew what happened to the drunks outside but I held my urge till daybreak, making sure my family jewels weren't swiped away while relieving myself.

We so enjoyed that outing that we decided to go big time backpacking, this time to the Rocky Mountains. It would take some planning. First, there was my age. I was 55 in 1986 but felt strong enough for the task. Then the two boys were in school. John, 24, was well into his Med School at the University of South Florida. Mark, 21, was in his third year of Architecture School at UVA. There were many backpacking options in the Rockies; we wanted to fish for trout, be away from tourists and enjoy solitude. Those requirements whittled the choice down to Wilderness areas.

Looking for solitary lakes with trout and away from crowds, reduced our choices to the Beartooth Wilderness in southwestern Montana, bordering the Yellowstone National Park. It was known as "Situation 1 grizzly habitat" meaning there were enough of them around to discourage most backpackers from visiting it. I researched the different glacial lakes that had been seeded with trout by the Montana Wildlife Dept.. With all that information in hand, I planned a one-week trek along selected lakes in the Beartooth Wilderness of Montana's Absaroka Range.

We flew into Billings, Montana, in late August, where we rented a car and drove down to Cooke City, on the northern border of Yellowstone National Park. We rented a room in one of the cabins of the Big Moose Resort, dropped the car off at the trailhead, and struck off with our 30 to 40-lb. backpacks toward the first of several lakes we

would visit that week. There were moments of pure joy along the way, sensing life in its proper perspective, seeing the spectacle of mountains putting on night clothes as the peaks darkened, and seeing the Milky Way at night. No world existed for any of us save the pure, grand, remote, abiding, enchanted world of mountains. I remember feeling for the first time the rapture of being alive.

Several spots we saw during that trip remain engraved in memory. One was a massif brooding over Lake Ouzel, where we spent the second night. A white mountain goat clinging to its sheer cliff the evening we got there came down to check up on us at our campsite later that night. Early next morning, as the sun caressed the top of the massif with its first rays, the rock, in silvered majesty, brooded over Lake Ouzel, offering its weathered face to the kiss of morning – a fleeting moment of glory. The thought of the awesome geological upheaval that had pushed it up overwhelmed me.

Another memorable episode was getting to Upper Lake Aero. The peaks in the high plateau soared like mammoth cairns to the gods. Ragged slabs of dirty, rose-tinged snow clung to the crevices, like bad patchwork by a do-it-yourself plasterer. We had to hop between shards and rocks, make stair steps on 45-degree slopes of corn snow, and pant up gray peaks, ridges and basalt-granite walls reaching for the sky. It was a wild, imposing, jagged wilderness and my "mountain goats" took me through the paces, unrelentingly "following the ridge", in a merciless search for height from which to dominate the panorama and search for the easiest – and sometimes only – way down to Lake Aero.

We proceeded along nameless ridges, testing and savoring the solitude and grandeur of the untouched mountain ranges, with their sober magnificent silences and the primeval here-I-am, the unspoken statement of creation. God hovered over the mountainscape in shrieking silence, and awe was in my every exhalation. There is a heroic quality to Beartooh hiking and few hikers are immune to their pre-Cambrian grandeur.

When we finally got there, the deep Upper Lake Aero was full of cutthroat but they weren't biting. Waking up the next morning I saw a family of mountain goats grazing a couple of feet beyond John and Mark's tent; a magnificent male four feet at the shoulders, its doe and two kids. When I called out to the boys to wake up and see the spectacle, the doe and her kids took off for the heights while the male stood its ground and merely stared at me for a while. When it felt all was clear, he followed his family without looking back. Magnificent animals!

We eventually got down to base camp and, after the usual pitcher of beer and Rocky Mountain oysters, proceeded on to savor the magnificence of Yellowstone. We gawked at herds of buffalo and got our fill of the most impressive geothermal manifestations on earth, from geysers to hot springs, fumaroles to mud pots.

 We then visited Cody, a small cowboy town 2 hours west of Yellowstone. We spent the night at the Irma Hotel, built by Buffalo Bill in 1904 and named after his youngest daughter. It featured restored Victorian style suites, and an impressive cherry wood-framed mirror behind the bar, a gift from Queen Victoria to Buffalo Bill. We visited the Museum, locally dubbed the 'Smithsonian of the West', with its great collection of firearms, a section on Indian artifacts and a wonderful western art section boasting original paintings and sculptures by Remington, Jackson and Russell, among others.

We had seen a lot of country in ten days and felt the grandeur of mountains and valleys, sated with the joy of solitary wandering. The best way to rekindle spirits is atop a crest, in the company of strong sons, in the threshold of heaven, where He is but a whisper away.

It was not the last backpacking trip we'd make. Two years later, in the summer of 1988, we decided to hike both the Wind River Range and our familiar Beartooth lakes. We flew to Salt Lake City, rented a car and drove to the trailhead in Pinedale, WY. John decided to bring his dog, Roy, along this time. The fishing in the Wind River lakes was not exceptional. I brought my harmonica along, as usual, and one night played a medley of golden oldies, like Lily *Marlene, Danny Boy, the Battle Hymn of the Republic,* followed by Basque, San Fermín ditties like *Uno de Enero,* *"Yo tenía una novia, alla en la montaña.." "Un estudiante a una niña le pidió.,"* ending the medley with a spirited rendition of the 7th Cavalry's Gary Owen battle hymn. The boys grumbled under their sleeping bags in the neighboring tent, refusing to join in.

On the way to Montana, we drove past the Grand Tetons, whose sexual allusion reminded me of the Spanish Conquistadors' "Punta Gorda" in Florida. Trailblazers have a decidedly bawdy sense of humor. We stopped for lunch at the Old Faithful Lodge in Yellowstone and noticed all the fire trucks dousing it. There was a monstrous fire in the Park and we were turned back by the fire rangers, having to go around the Norris blockade to get to our destination, Cooke City, where we spent the night at a motel. The fires raged across the mountain, fires than would eventually crest and roar down the valley to burn a couple of buildings in town. The town's proud title of "Snowmobile Capital of the U.S.A." seemed oddly incongruous.

Our old friend Krum suggested we visit Lake Stephanie, which was supposed to be jumping with cutthroat. The shortcut to the Lake proposed by John meant climbing a 35° slope, an effort which almost did me in. But it was well worth it; every cast in the small lake was a cutthroat strike. It got to be boring, but we ate well that night, Mark, as usual, ensconced in the best shelter around.

 Later in the hike, "thunder thighs" Mark[101], who, up to that moment, had served as point for our group, came running back warning us that Roy had roused a bear. We dropped our packs and desperately searched for a tree to climb. The bear, it turned out, was a mother moose that came chasing after Roy for spooking its doe. Trying to escape the threat, Roy retreated towards us and hid behind the trunk of our tree. He wouldn't stop barking at the irate moose, despite our urging. We remained treed for a good half hour, until the moose, tired of trying to hoof Roy, just took off with its doe.

When we came off the trail, we visited the underwhelming Custer's Memorial, in a desolate hill south of Billings. The only interesting thing about that visit was our guide, who claimed to be a half brother of Marlon Brando - both sons of an Indian woman who had been buried a week earlier, with great pomp and ceremony.

John Campbell wrote in his "Power of Myth" that "the only vision lives far from mankind, out in the great loneliness, and can be reached only through suffering." There is a principle I like to call the "Conservation of Pain Theorem," never more operative than when climbing in and out of those lakes in the high Rockies, where the exhilaration of descent is balanced by the agony of having to climb back out the next day, nor more manifest than in Roy's gorging himself on freedom after being released from the confining airplane kennel. Life seems to seek its level amidst universal pain-joy counterpoints, ineffably seeding the river of entropy with unexpected islands of order and joy.

That trip, like the others, brought back the ecstasy of free space.

---

[101] He had spent that winter as a rescue ranger in a ski resort in New England and had exercised his thighs to the point where his hiking pants were almost too tight.

At night, the awesome hush of galaxies and the simple hiss of distance spoke in rustles of eternity. As ever, the glacier-sculpted Beartooths evoked the sense of nature's forces, and the night sky, shimmering in the untrammeled expanses, sang out its limpid sound of healing silence, with ablutions of solitude and peace. It felt good to be alive.

Chapter 14

The Sundowning Years

"Kipling refused to turn his back on any man's hearthstone. I'll never forget the wonder and delight that went to build my own."
JML

As my years in the Defense community progressed, my career as a Nuclear Physicist evolved into something more like a Rocket Scientist's. Much smaller miss distances were achievable with advanced guidance systems, which meant defensive nuclear warheads had become obsolete. I remember working for the Patriot program when the Desert Storm war broke out. Our air defense missile was pitted against Sadam Hussein's Russian SCUD missiles in the Kuwaiti struggle, simply because there was no other fielded defense system half capable of stopping the short range missile threat. The Patriot missile performed respectably well. But not perfectly.

I set about studying ways of improving the missile's effectiveness by foregoing the ground based radar's guidance altogether and equipping the missile with a homing device with a smaller directed-fragment warhead. The decision for the proposed improvements ultimately rested with Raytheon, the Patriot missile's Prime contractor. But the monolithic, organization, with vested interests in its ground based radar, was averse to radical changes, particularly if suggested by outsiders.

213

Disappointed by their parochial attitude, I started working on an Internal Research and Development (IRAD) study to design and field a completely different, warhead-less defense missile, equipped with an IR seeker, with a guidance system so unique and effective that it could theoretically hit and kill either incoming ballistic missiles or aircraft, foregoing the need for a ground-based radar guidance. It would be small and portable, a theater Commander's dream.

I had come full circle in my career; from the Sprint defense missile with a nuclear warhead to the advanced Patriot's non-nuclear, directed fragment warhead, and finally to THAADS, the Theater High Altitude Area Defense System, an IR-guided, warhead-less missile designed to run into and destroy any incoming target, missile or aircraft. The evolution was complete.

The community eventually warmed up to the idea and the Defense Department's ABM organization let a proposal to define, develop and field such a system. It would take years to finally field the system, eventually named MEADS, an acronym for Medium Extended Air Defense System. I would, by then, have retired as the program's Technical Director and only read in the press about its trials, tribulations and final success.

It was a fun and exciting professional life, always trying to come up with novel concepts, pushing the defense technology to its limits. I was glad to have gone through all those gyrations in my life, from the shipping business to the grueling nine years of University studies, to the brief teaching job and ending with the almost thirty years in the Defense business.

But, fun and challenging as work was, I always managed to leave it at the office when I came home, to my cleaner, greener world. We were all getting older and wiser and time, like aged wine, made life taste that much sweeter. I was old enough to realize that the gift of this broad-shouldered, ruggedly handsome land was wholly unmerited. Its

214

impressive majesty still awes me today, like it did when I first landed on its shores, pregnant with promise of new beginnings. I still remember the bigness of its sky, the roar of its thunder, even the unexpected jolts of its static electricity – everything in America is big. And such a beautiful country, the name it goes by in China.

And the many haunting strains I learned along the way, some of which I've spent years acquiring countless cassettes and CDs trying to  recapture the now lost but fondly remembered Bach strain, which I believe to be a Partita, or was it a Sonata?

Or the hauntingly peaceful Allegretto movement that follows the terrible storm in Beethoven's Pastoral Symphony, a melody I first heard in College and later transmogrified into the lullaby I sang to put my children and grandchildren to sleep, with the whimsically childish and nonsensical lyrics:

"Ete mi noñi, cochín, cochín, cochón.."

which they learned to love and half expect, before their nightly sojourn into sleep.

And how forget the smell of new-mown hay in the lovely, summer-yellow meadows of Navarre? Or the sweet scent of ripe, wild strawberries that blanketed the slopes of Menditxuri, the White Mountain hulking over the ancestral village of Burguete, which my two sons still love to jog up to?

215

If smells and sounds can so vividly bring back the spirit of days gone by, the haunting beauty of words never fails to touch some inmost chord in me because they speak of things one deeply feels about yet cannot wholly express. Such quatrains as Lope de Vega's *Soledades* remain particularly poignant:

A mis soledades voy,
To my solitudes I go,
De mis soledades vengo,
From them I come,
Porque para andar conmigo
Because to walk with me
Me bastan mis pensamientos.
My thoughts suffice.

No sé qué tiene mi aldea
I know not what my hamlet has
Donde vivo y donde muero
wherein I live and die,
Que con venir de mí mismo
but by coming from myself
No puedo venir de más lejos.
I can come from no farther.

Or the no less bewitching words of the Spanish mystic, San Juan de la Cruz, strung out in painful verses, like so many saints in those Greco paintings:

No me mueve, mi Dios, para quererte
Neither your promised heaven, Lord,
El cielo que me tienes prometido,
nor the fear of hell
Ni me mueve el infierno tan temido,
move me to love you, or
Para dejar, por eso, de quererte.
keep me from loving you.

Muévesme a tu amor en tal manera
Even if there were no
Que aunque no hubiese cielo, yo te amara,
heaven I'd still love you, and fear you,
Y aunque no hubiese infierno, te temiera.
were there were no hell.

No me tienes que dar porque te quiera,
So give me naught for my love,
Que aunque cuanto espero no esperara,
Lord, for even without a reward
Lo mismo que te quiero, te quisiera.
I'd still love you.

Translations, like comparisons, are odious. So the reader will just have to learn Spanish to get the full and ineffable feel of that mystic's poem.

And like unfinished symphonies, reminiscences must, like this one, be brief and end abruptly.

Exciting as those years were, my post retirement years have been even more joyous and rewarding. Retirement, aptly called *Jubilación* in Spanish, i.e. jubilation, is an apposite name for that state of euphoric triumph. I feel lucky to be able to enjoy these sunset years, or as my son

Mark and, later, my dear father- in- law called them "the sundowning years."

I have a lot of people to thank for this jubilation, starting with Dad who set my keel of honor straight early on; my mother, Achi, whose unstinting love, tenderness and trust instilled in me my love of people; to Jac Chambliss, who gave me his daughter and an undying fondness for words; to his daughter Ann whose love and devotion were manifest from the first day we met and stood by me through thick and thin[102] or, as we promised in our altar vows, in sickness and in health.

And how forget Ted Ryberg, without whose help and encouragement I probably wouldn't have attended College in the United States; and Drs. Mara and Tilley, and all those good people who urged me on, despite my many shortfalls. And the list goes on until my cup runneth empty of gratitude.

Besides the wonderful years of tennis, gardening, golf, babysitting grandchildren and writing, there were those wonderful vacations in exotic places. Particularly memorable was the trip to the Far East, which included New Zealand[103], Australia and the Philippines. We found New Zealand to be a beautiful country with 3½ million friendly people and 80 million sheep. I found Australia ho-hum but revisiting the Philippines after a half century's absence was unforgettable.

I was impressed by the mass of humanity there, and the traffic everywhere. When I studied geography as a boy, the Islands' population was a mere 18 million; today, it's grown to over 110 million. After visiting friends in Manila, Ann and I spent a few days in the little

---

[102] Even making my bed up every single day of our married life

[103] I've often threatened to move to New Zealand when some cordially disliked politician came close to winning the Presidency.

dreamy island of Boracay, off the northwestern tip of Panay, the island where I was born. No more than three miles long, it was bordered by pristine, sugar-white sand, lined with coconut trees and almost untouched by tourists. If one were to picture paradise, there would be no closer depiction of it. The trip in a taxi to Iloilo, on the opposite tip of Panay, was sobering. We drove past two AK-47-toting natives guarding the desolate country road and wondered if we'd be kidnapped. We weren't.

Except for the mass of people and traffic jams, Iloilo remained the same. We visited our old Elizalde home during the war, now a Philippine IRS branch office. It was disheartening to see the missing scrolled mahogany stairway down whose banisters Luis and I used to slide race[104]. Also gone was the flimsy iron ladder Luis and I used to climb to the house's roof to watch the fireworks during the war.

The Plaza Libertad was still there, as was the San Jose Church where I served Mass as a young acolyte, and its choir, where I used to sing Christmas carols. The Hospital San Pablo where I was born was still there, as was my old San Agustin High School, now a University. But the beach in which we used to swim, where the nuns once wrote the life-saving message "No more Japs in City" was gone, as was the small airfield where we once set the last of the Japanese gasoline drums on fire. Now there was only a *bidonville*, a jumble of tin and cardboard huts stacked all the way down to the sea, where the swelling population lived. The country had literally gone to the dogs. It was during that visit that I finally learned that one definitely can't go home again.

And then there were the two trips to Mexico, the second foolishly repeating our first trip's itinerary. The bus to Dolores was

---

[104] Imelda Marcos, wife of the then President, took a fancy to it and simply requisitioned it.

219

memorable.

Neither cardiologists nor psychiatrists make a very good living in Mexico, where a shrug of the shoulders is the natives' reflex response to stress. Visitors to this relaxed, laid-back country soon learn to allow a little extra time for contingencies – which inevitably arise.

Our first brush with this laissez-faire life style came as Ann and I were getting ready to leave Mexico City for the hinterlands. We had planned to drive to San Miguel de Allende to spend the next few days visiting this quaint Colonial relic. Arrangements had been made for a rental car to be delivered that afternoon to the Hotel El Cortés[105], where we were staying.

Not having heard from the car rental folks and growing increasingly skeptical that our car would be delivered at all, we decided, on the uninspired spur of the moment, to proceed by bus and later rent a car in San Miguel. Undaunted, we headed for the Flecha Amarilla ticket counter at the bus station. Although that Company offered only Second Class accommodations, it was the last and only departure to San Miguel that afternoon.

We were instructed to board the bus to Dolores, scheduled to leave at around 4:15 that afternoon from a yet-to-be-determined quay, somewhere between ramps 19 and 21. The $3.50 fare for the four-hour trip should have warned me of the odyssey ahead. We parked ourselves on a bench at the main terminal, amidst a sea of long-suffering Mexican *paisanos* milling about desultorily from ramp to ramp, earnestly clutching their belongings. Occasionally, when a bus pulled up on one of the quays, a wave of suppressed excitement swept over the crowd,

---

[105] It amazed me that any self-respecting Mexican entrepreneur would name his place of business after the much-maligned Conquistador.

followed by a determined shuffling and shoving. When one of the bus's drivers shouted "Querétaro!" a distinct sigh of relief arose from the impatient crowd. I figured that must have been home to a lot of those Sunday tourists.

Totally devoid of markings, a nondescript bus suddenly loomed out of the fumes and surreptitiously slipped into ramp 19. The Yellow Arrow (*Flecha Amarilla)* logo was barely discernible under layers of dust and caked mud. Sticking his head out of the window, its driver announced sonorously, but just above the din: "Dolores!"

We boarded it with relieved alacrity. I had an eerie sensation that we were boarding the last boat to the Molokai leprosarium. The two front-row seats we chose were directly behind the driver's. We settled down on the half-empty conveyance's rickety seats, relaxed, and looked forward to a peaceful ride to San Miguel.

My dreamy content was abruptly shattered when the driver leaned out of his window and bellowed: "Santa Ana!" A veritable wave of anxious peasants stormed the bus. Young and old streamed past us, grimly clutching mementos of a Sunday spree at the Capital, including the proverbial chickens, which added measurably to the general cacophony. When every seat was taken, the driver expanded the itinerary by advertising yet another intermediate stop. These inspired announcements had an electrifying effect on the waiting populace, who, I suspect, half anticipated the impromptu announcements. The bus' aisle soon disappeared under a compacted mass of amorphous humanity, the more agile of whom decided to share the luggage racks with the *serapes* and the chickens. The ancient conveyance groaned audibly under the assault. Finally, the perverse grin that had started to spread across the driver's face told me that his stevedoring feat was finally accomplished.

And none too soon for I was by now literally pinned down by several young Mexicans leaning on my head, shoulders and arm rest, they themselves pinioned by the faceless mass pressing down on them. I was surprised by the quietude of all those Mexican babies around me, refusing to cry or whimper despite the obvious discomfort. Across the aisle, an addled grandmother fussed with one of her shoes, asking no one in particular the whereabouts of her missing stocking. The suspicious glances she cast in my direction began to make me nervous. For the rest, the teeming bus fell eerily silent, as if reverting to a survival instinct of languid serenity and pliant resignation in the face of onrushing adversity.

The bus finally coughed itself alive and slowly wove its way out of the terminal. Before long, it was hurtling down the highway, on its way north to Querétaro. From the moment he turned on the ignition, the driver engaged in lively conversation with his Purser, who sat on the jump seat next to him. Peals of laughter followed mention of daring and unprintable exploits of "*el Chaquetas*" and "*el Lobo*", nicknames of fellow drivers in their disreputable *Flecha Amarilla* fleet.

Midway to Querétaro the bus stopped at a toll gate, where an officious-looking inspector attempted to board the sagging bus for a head count. Unable to breech the wall of humanity at the door, he had to take the driver's word for what was, all too obviously, a flagrant underestimate of his passenger count. The bus proceeded on its wayward way, with much giggling at the wheel, at the expense of the frustrated official.

Barreling down the progressively-deteriorating highway, we overtook several other Flecha Amarilla buses. Recognizing one another, the conductors rolled down their windows and made lewd signs to each other and, with puerile glee, dared one another to a drag race. The two maniacs then floored their accelerators and for the next dozen miles, proceeded on low, earth orbits, two buses bounding side by side along a potted road hardly wide enough to accommodate one. They roared on at speeds that would have made Earnhardt drool. Meanwhile, an ominous pall had descended on the passengers aboard. Their dilated pupils frozen in distended stares, jaw muscles grimly set, white knuckles gripping arm rests, all emoted a bottomless feeling akin to terror. The addled grandmother across the aisle began to cackle nervously, still eyeing me suspiciously every chance she got.

The Purser, who went by the officious Spanish title of "Sobrecargo,"(Purser), was mockingly addressed by the driver as the "Sobre-estorbo," (super-bother). For suffering the play on words and laughing at his boss' corny jokes, he was allowed to drive the bus during brief intervals between unscheduled stops, even though he, in all likelihood, didn't have a driver's license. Sitting at the wheel and fairly bursting with self importance, we overheard him comment on the erratic behavior of the brakes. The driver acknowledged having noticed the brakes' intermittent fading, but assured the Purser there was nothing to worry about, that he'd have them checked on his return trip to Mexico City. The ominous admission was seismic. Only the gathering dusk on the desolation outside talked me out of getting off the bus, right there and then.

Like the ones before it, the next stop came unannounced. It happened at the crest of a dark, windswept hill, a pimple on an unfeeling landscape in the middle of nowhere. Three young blades in their cups staggered onto the bus and, somehow, managed to slip past the dozing Purser. Clambering up on the luggage racks over chickens and sleeping occupants, they crawled their way toward the back of the bus, giggling and mildly barfing as they went. Noticing the deftly-executed maneuver through his rear-view mirror, the driver ordered the *Sobre-estorbo* to go after them and collect their fare. After negotiating the luggage rack route twice, the subdued Purser returned minutes later, lamely admitting that they could only muster five pesos between them.

Exploding in rich invective, the driver slammed on the brakes with irate authority. As the bus screeched to a dead stop, some passengers came spilling out of the racks, chickens flew cackling about the bus, and the grandmother lost her other stocking. Amidst a barrage of choice expletives from the livid driver, the three revelers stumbled out into the pitch black night, unceremoniously dumped in the middle of absolutely nowhere. As if on cue, the expression "up the creek without a paddle" came bubbling up.

It was almost midnight when we finally rattled into the derelict bus station in San Miguel. I couldn't help feeling that I had been transported back in time to the days of Cortés. The trip's improbable happenings reminded me of that other even more implausible event, four hundred years earlier, when a handful of ragged Conquistadors took over an insouciant and distracted empire. It was perhaps only appropriate that the first gesture of shedding that Colonial yoke should have taken place three-hundred odd years later, in a town called Dolores, (*"pains"* in Spanish). I couldn't help chuckling at the coincidence between those national birth pangs and the more prosaic ones riding the *Flecha Amarilla* bus to Dolores.

One of the more memorable trips Ann and I made was visiting all the lodges in the National Parks of the Rocky Mountains, in the company of my brother Luis and his wife Maite. We converged on Las Vegas where we enjoyed the Irish show, River Dance, that first night. We then proceeded to East Grand Canyon National Park and stayed at the magnificent El Tovar Lodge. All four of us went river rafting with a Hualapai Indian guide the next morning, where we got rained on and hailed upon. Coming out of the river at the end of the ride and dashing up a hill to relieve ourselves, I got hit by the first of five shocks from my implanted defibrillator, just as Luis was pronouncing: "*Picha Española nunca mea sola.*"

We thoroughly enjoyed that month-long vacation, Luis and I

laughing while reminiscing olden times, Ann and Maite in the back of the car, talking women talk while enjoying Andrea Bocceli's *Romanza*. During the rest of the trip we visited Zion, Bryce, Jackson Hole, Yellowstone[106], Glacier, Coeur d'Alene, Salish Lodge in Snoqualmie, near Seattle, to visit John and Mark, and finally San Francisco, where we parted company. It was a trip of a lifetime for both couples.

The incident I remember most about that trip was arriving at East Glacier Lodge early one afternoon and renting a cart and golf gear at their Golf Shop. We were advised by the Pro to avoid looking for lost balls in the woods around fairways 3, 4 & 5 because there was a family of visiting grizzlies residing there. Sure enough, when we lost a ball in the woods around fairway 4, I chuckled, noticing Luis gripping a 5-iron as to dear life, as if that were any good against a grizzly!

We vacationed in Spain every other year. Some of those trips weren't vacations at all, but funerals, like Mom's, when she passed away at age 86 and our burying her ashes in the family plot in Burguete, one wintry, snowy day. Among the people who showed up at her funeral was my cousin Santi, whom I hadn't seen since my days in Pamplona in 1947.My brother Luis also passed away from lung cancer at age 72, followed, shortly after, by his son Javier, after a lifetime of suffering with diabetes.

My younger sister Maite was in her twenties when she joined the Opus Dei, in whose houses of Madrid and Las Rozas she has lived and worked. She loves walking, like her aunt Beatriz, and is always in good health, living only to help other people. Her kindness, good sense

---

[106] Only young, 12-year old pines remained after the 1988 fire we had witnessed on our last backpacking trip there.

and diplomacy always remind me of Mom. She was a godsend to Mom when she got sick and to Maite Agudo, when she came down with recurring depressions.

My older sister, Mari Blanca stayed with her Order of Sisters of Charity for a few years. Favoring missionary work, she was sent to the high country of Peru to work with Indians in Puno, on Lake Titicaca, and subsequently to a school in the coastal town of Mollendo. She got in trouble with the authorities for contesting the threatened closure of her school. She was subsequently sent to Haiti to do mission work there and when she returned to her home base in Puerto Rico, she decided to leave the Order and start one of her own, more attuned to proselytizing than to nursing.

We visited her on her 60th. Anniversary of becoming a nun, and were impressed by her adoring following. She is 82 now and still going strong. Her sister in law, Maite, used to say that Saints have always been misunderstood. I can understand that.

Ann used to take her students on short trips to Greece and Italy. I accompanied her once and was startled when, to my chagrin and the kids' hilarity, a belly dancer in an Athenian taverna playfully buried my face between her sweaty breasts. Ann also visited Egypt and China on her own, I being busy at work at the time.

But we managed to travel to Europe almost every year. We enjoyed traveling with grandchildren and showing them places we knew and loved, hoping they, too, would learn to appreciate the finer things in life. We took

226

grandson Jac out West when he turned nine, and Will to visit castles in Spain, when he turned 10. Alexandra went to Paris on a women-only trip, with her mother and Ann when she turned 10, while I went on an all-male family trip to my son-in-law, John Shubert's fishing camp in a Canadian lake, west of Ontario, where the young ones ran around naked all day and learned to play Mus.

And how forget the Tapas trip to Spain with my two sons in 2005, a two-week jaunt visiting only tapas bars, mostly in northern Spain. The highlight of that trip was living practically inside the Barrio Viejo of San Sebastian, where the best tapas in the world are found. We slept in a seedy Pension right in the middle of the drinking village so we didn't have to drive at all, simply eat, drink and walk up to bed. We didn't visit a single restaurant during that whole trip, eating simply *chocolate con churros* for breakfast and tapas bar-hopping the rest of the day. There were glorious *morcillas* and *boquerones* and *gambas al ajillo,* to name but a few of the Basque delicacies.

But our most memorable trip of all was to celebrate our 50th.Wedding Anniversary in the Hotel Loizu, in Burguete, with our whole brood, all 16 of us. I took them to Ortzanzurieta, the tallest Pyrenean peak in the vicinity, then to the castle of Javier,

where we picnicked on the castle grounds, and, of course, to the Fiestas de San Juan in Burguete, where sons and grandchildren jumped over the bonfires, following an ancient ritual. There were visits to the nearby Abbey of Roncesvalles, of such fond memories, both Achi's and mine. But what pleased me most was listening to my grandsons talking about one day running the bulls in San Fermin, like their grandfather and fathers had, so many years ago.

Besides fun trips, there were other enjoyable pastimes after retirement. I picked up golf, when tennis became too strenuous. I've thoroughly enjoyed the game, having met nicer people at my little 9-hole Winter Park Golf course than I did in almost 30 years of professional life. I surprise myself smiling every time I drive by the charming course in the heart of Winter Park, the way I used to smile when driving to work in the outskirts of Denver, on seeing the snow-capped Rockies beyond.

Cousin Alberto and his sister Alicia came to visit once. Neither had travelled beyond the occasional short shopping trips to Pamplona. And so the transatlantic flights (they came twice!), the hot-air balloon ride with Alberto, and the cruise to Cancun, Mexico, were totally out of the ordinary for the two country kin. It was fun watching Alberto snoring while taking his inveterate siesta in a park hammock in Cancun, surrounded by bemused children. It was only my camcorder film of the event that convinced him of his sonorous sleeping.

And then there was writing. Ever since Jac Chambliss gave me a copy of his essay "The Psalmist," I've been in love with the beauty of words. No sooner had I retired than I started writing about my war memoirs. Published in Manila under the title "Rising Sun Blinking," it ran out of print and had a second run, since. Years later, I had it published in the States. Once, some Hollywood script writer showed interest in making a movie of it but nothing came of it.

I cannot fail to mention the joy of grandchildren, whom I consider the extension of myself and the living testimony of Ann's and my genes. We have been blessed with eight of them, all loving, intelligent and fun kids. Laura and John Shubert, have blessed us with two fine boys, Jac and Will, and a girl, the lovely Alexandra. John and Mark, happily married to Rebecca and Deirdre, live and work in Seattle. We've all heard of proud Jewish mothers bragging about "my son, the doctor." Well, we happen to have two! They have given us another five talented and handsome grandchildren; Sophia, Lucas, Jac, Matthew and Olivia. I find no greater joy than being in their company and seeing glimmers of their bright future. May their lives be as full and exciting as mine, and, as the lovely Irish prayer goes:

May the road rise to meet you,
May the wind be always at your back,
May the sun shine warm upon your face,
The rains fall softly on your fields,
And until we meet again
May God hold you in the palm of His hand.

Chapter 15

Querencia[107]

"It is natural for a man to like to live at home, and to live long elsewhere without a sense of exile is not good for his moral integrity"
Winds of Doctrine
George Santayana

I quote that Santayana thought with the same dubious enjoyment of biting a sore tooth. I find some solace in the sentence that follows: "It is right to feel a greater kinship and affection for what lies nearest to oneself," and with the angst of stray human driftwood, I cry: "*Ubi bene ibi patria!*" trying to remind myself that I love this blonde giant shore like my own. But humming fiercely, deep down, is the sonnet I once wrote in my African years:

"Shall I see them again, blood brothers of mine?
...How strong the pull, how clear the call,
how deep the utter beauty of my land, so well beloved!"

My neighbor Jack Lane recently asked me whether, after all these years, I felt more American than Spanish. I had to stop and think. I've lived in this beautiful country for over half a century. It has been good to me, and I have served it well. Indeed, my eyes still water when I sing "The Battle Hymn of the Republic" or "Oh beautiful for spacious

---

[107] Spanish: Inclination of man or beast to return to the place where they were bred and raised.

231

skies.." because, deep down, the lyrics move me. But after mulling over his query, I answered: "I feel Basque. I fill that out in every Census form I've ever filled out over the years. And so, despite the Latin cry of *Ubi bene, ibi patria*, I am and always have been a Basque.

I'd always been intrigued by my people, the Basques. From my youngest years Mom used to talk about how her grandfather and his forbears had gone by the noble title of Señores de Agorreta. I once visited the old family manor house, grandmother's ancestral lair in the hamlet of Agorreta, in the hinterlands of Navarre. While there, I discovered an old manuscript dated 1526 stating that, even back then, the House of Agorreta had existed "since time immemorial." I decided, then and there, to research the origin of my people.

Following is a synopsis[108] of that research:

A few segregated pockets of human populations exists in the world today whose origins have long intrigued anthropologists. The Basques, whose roots are lost in prehistoric mists, belong to one such race. Over the years there had been many quaint theories about these people's origins, from survivors of the ill-fated Atlantis, to stragglers of the lost tribe of Israel. But recent linguistic and genetic investigations confirm the even more startling thesis that the Basques are stragglers of the first group of Cro-Magnon to venture out of the Middle East during the middle Paleolithic, in the Pandorf Interstadial, forty thousand years ago, to displace the Neanderthals and settle Europe.

Their non Indo-European language has always been a mystery. But words embedded in their language today for rudimentary tools such as *aitzkorra* (ax), *aitzkur* (spade) and *aitzto* (knife), whose radix *aitz* means stone, hint at the material their Stone Age forbears must have used to fashion these tools. A Spanish linguist[109], who broke the

---

[108] Preface to "*The Lords of Navarre*," Jose Maria Lacambra-Loizu, iUniverse, 2004

[109] Jorge Alonso García, "*Desciframiento de la Lengua Ibérico-Tartésica*," Fundación

Iberian hieroglyphic cipher, proved that the inscriptions in Iberian vases, tombstones and lead tablets unearthed in eastern Spain represent Basque words, written in archaic Phoenician and proto-Greek alphabets. This leads to the intriguing hypothesis that Basques, read "Iberians", come from the Caucasus. Over two thousand years ago Egyptian[110], Greek[111] and Roman[112] sources identified the inhabitants of the southeastern foothills of the Caucasus as Iberians. Strabo's and Pliny's commentaries further aver that, during Roman times, Iberian was widely spoken in a vast region in southwestern France which the Romans called Aquitaine, "the watery one."

Combined with the ice-aged words fossilized in their language, this wealth of clues strongly suggests an Iberian (read Basque) ice-age migration from the Caucasus to Western Europe and their eventual crossing of the Pyrenees to settle in the peninsula that bears their name today. Corroborating this conjecture is the recent genetic sleuthing[113] of Basque mitochondrial DNA, confirming that just such a migration took place some forty thousand years ago, right about the time of the first Cro-Magnon incursion into Europe.

Inspired by a fierce spirit of independence, these endogamous stragglers managed to retain their archaic language, their relic racial characteristics and their original blood genotype[114]. It is startling to realize that the Neolithic artists of those handsome cave paintings in

---

Tartesos, 1997

[110] Ptolemy, *Geography*, Book 5, Ch. 10

[111] Strabo *Geography*, 11.1.5, Loeb

[112] Pliny, Book 3, Ch. 3, 29

[113] Luigi Cavalli-Sforza, *Genes, Peoples and Languages*, North Point Press, 2000

[114] The preponderance of the O⁻ blood genotype among them occurs in a far greater proportion than in any other living population group on earth.

Chauvet. Lascaux, Niaux, Isturitz and Altamira were Basque. It is equally intriguing to conjecture that listening to spoken Basque today may be like listening to a scratchy millennial tape recording of our Cro-Magnon ancestors.

As this band of Basque hunters finally surface into history, we see them rub reluctant elbows with Celts, join the Roman Legions in the Rhine, tangle with Charlemagne at Roncevaux and fight North African Muslims in battles from Covadonga to *al-Andalús*, always fiercely defending their beloved Vascon valleys in the Pyrenean uplands.

At the cusp of the Age of Chivalry, an Agorreta participated in jousts, took the Cross in Lionheart's Crusade, and wooed a Moorish princess whose brother he later helped defeat in the turning point battle of Navas de Tolosa. Later still, now in the thick of the middle Ages, another Agorreta crosses swords with the Black Prince at Crecy and later fights under the Englishman's banner at Nájera. Finally, during the twilight years of the Vascon kingdom of Navarre, several Agorretas attain Royal Judgeships, serve as Seneschals to kings and bear brave lances under Cesare Borgia.

Although that chronicle ended on the eve of the annexation of a once fiercely independent Vasconia to the nascent kingdom of Spain, the following epilogue of the same book reminisces on a particularly nostalgic visit I made to the mountain country of my forebears:

The two-mile stretch between Burguete and Roncesvalles is a hauntingly beautiful beech-lined lane. It is now eerily quiet, with its dreams of fern, velvety moss and patches of wild strawberries growing along its shallow ditches. Unexpected shafts of sunlight shine through the canopy of beech and silver fir, dappling the lichen-stained Pilgrim's

234

Cross that guards the southern approaches to Roncesvalles. In a rare moment of quiet epiphany, I am swept by the feeling of *déjà vu*, uncannily reminded that I had been there, countless centuries ago, marching shoulder-to-shoulder with kindred Vascon warriors on our way to punish the Frank.

At the foot of the lofty mountain the Romans called *Summo Pyreneo* is Orreaga, or 'place of thorns'. The French also call it Roncevaux, valleys of thorns, for the flower of their knighthood once fought there and lost a thorny battle which minstrels and troubadours immortalized in The Song of Roland, a medieval *chançon de geste*.

Among an odd assortment of buildings of patently ancient architecture is a narrow stone church dating back to Sancho el Fuerte's thirteenth century, in whose loophole a small brass bell hangs. One can still hear its snow-muffled chimes carrying over the fog-bound mountains, guiding pilgrims out of the dark forests into the welcome warmth and safety of the Hospice of Roncesvalles. The hospice was once held in the same high esteem as those of Jerusalem, Rome and Santiago, manned by the first monastic Military Hospitalier Order in Christendom. Their charter was to care for the pilgrims during their hazardous Pyrenean crossing, protecting them from bears, wolves and marauding bandits.

The unmistakable sound of Gregorian chant wafts out of what appears to be yet another Thirteenth Century chapel. Inside is a dimly lit, incense-choked gothic chapel of simple elegance and grace. Behind its main altar are ornately-carved armchairs on which seven sleepy-eyed Canons are ensconced, singing an ancient homophonic Latin chant that rolls gently off the stark granite walls.

When they are through singing, I approach the altar and collar one of the Canons before he can disappear into the refectory. I have detained Don Agapito, the Royal Collegiate's official historian. Recognizing me as Mrs. Agorreta's grandson, he takes me by the arm and leads me up a dark, winding stairwell, through a long corridor and into a large, ill-lit room. It has the musty feel of a small private museum, incunabula and reliquaries untidily strewn about. Picking up an ancient mace with a worm-bitten handle and three attached spiked iron balls, the curate explains that Sancho el Fuerte once used it to break the chains encircling Miramamolin's tent during the epic battle of Navas de Tolosa in the year 1212.

He sat down to explain how the Romans used this road and the pass of Roncesvalles to move armies back and forth from Gaul, chasing Celts. The Romans, he said, left only their dead in these mountains they called the *Saltus Vasconum*. He then pulled an old leather-bound volume on whose front cover was the faded, gold-embossed Latin inscription: *De Bello Civili, Libro I,* and under it *J. Caesar.* Opening it to a dog-eared page, he starts reading, translating from Latin into Spanish as he went:

"Vascon men are as skillful at ambushing others as at avoiding ambuscades. They conduct their military operation with great ease and order, launching impetuous attacks with dispersed platoons, without distinction of position or rank. When obliged to cede, they retreat and escape to regroup again in a different place. They fight with a short, double edged sword, an offensive weapon which we Romans have copied from them and adopted as our own. They launch their spears with formidable accuracy

The horses of their cavalry know how to bend their knees when needed. Two riders mount each horse, one jumping off to fight on foot while the other remains mounted. They have absolute disdain for death and are prodigal with their lives in combat. Neither hunger nor thirst bothers them, nor cold confines them, nor does heat fatigue them. Their only regret is to reach a useless old age."

Caesar's commentary impressed me. Don Agapito added that the Romans used to recruite these mountain tribesmen as volunteers to serve as cohorts in the Roman Legions. Tacitus[115], he said, wrote about Basque cohorts fighting gallantly in the Rhine against the Germans.

 He then led me into a large, square enclosure on the first floor, just beyond the cloister. Its ceiling was supported by an elaborate Gothic ribbing, its magnificent vault rising some eighty feet above the granite floor. Light streamed into the hall from a huge rosette window framing a magnificent stained-glass rendition of a medieval battle. "This," said the curate "is the pantheon of King Sancho el Fuerte of Navarre. He defeated the Moors in the battle of Navas de Tolosa in 1212, shown in the rosette window. The recumbent figure on this sarcophagus is a faithful replica of el Fuerte. He was a veritable giant, measuring some two and a quarter meters in height. That's over seven and half feet tall. And those rusty chains you see hanging over the massive granite altar are the very chains that once ringed the tent of the Moorish Caliph, Miramamolín, whom Sancho defeated in that battle. They have been the emblem of Navarre ever since and are now part of Spain's coat of arms."

I remained silent, awed by the realization that all this was part of my very own heritage. The tour had come to an end. He walked me out to the door and bade me farewell: "God be with you, pilgrim," he said, disappearing in the dark halls of his historic dwelling.

Hopping back in my car, I drove south, past rolling hills and green pastures, headed for my ancestral home in the town of Agorreta. The hamlet of Agorreta was perched on the edge of a sawed-off hill overlooking the road. I maneuvered the car up the narrow rise, inching

---

[115] Tacitus, The Histories, Book 4, Ch.33.

the vehicle toward the hamlet's square, parking the car directly in front of a large house that absolutely reeked of age. This was *Jaureguizar*, the old palace. To my right, a few dozen paces up the rise, sat a massive granite building brooding over the hamlet. This had to be *Gasteluzar*, the old castle. Breaking the monotony of its four walls were narrow slits through which arrows must have once been shot in self defense.

I have seen many manorial fortresses like *Gasteluzar* before, but *Jaureguizar* simply took my breath away. It was a grand old *caserío*, simple as all first ideas, primitive like all rough drafts. Its coarsely-hewn stones gave the mansion a certain unpretentious nobility and grandeur. The large two-story building with its swayback roof just sat there with a pained look of age about it, almost as if each stone's once-fond affection for its neighboring stone had waned, wearied of the weight and togetherness of eons. A feeling of age clung to everything about it, as if Time, in a moment of weakness, had chosen to spare it, tucking it away in one of its cobwebbed back rooms. Though not a ruin, the building flirted dangerously with the idea.

A crumbly escutcheon was sculpted on the façade of the house, just above the brass-studded front door. Two inverted crescent moons, heraldic arms earned fighting Moors in two different battles, graced two of its quadrants. I felt a shiver of pride on realizing that I had just touched the sarcophagus of the stalwart king with whom one of my ancestors was said to have fought in those battles.

 The old lady caretaker answered the door and let me in after identifying myself. Beyond a heavy oak door was a large basement that must have once served as stables for a sizeable herd of cows and horses. Along its ceiling were corpulent beams of dark, coarsely hewn oak, visibly bowed with age. In my mind's eye I could almost see a dozen men-at-arms being outfitted for battle in that huge basement, receiving their final marching orders from the Lord of the manor.

The caretaker led me up the main double-back stairs to a hall lined with a dozen bedrooms. They were empty now, their tall ceilings and wainscoted walls mute reminders of the manorial wealth the owners must have once enjoyed. At the western end of the long hallway was a large dining room, once probably the Great Hall. I could almost hear the now-stilled voices of the many festive receptions held there, whispered love avowals of long-ago trysts, even sobs for loved ones lost in battle, all haunting the place, wrapping themselves around me.

On a bookshelf along one of the walls, sagging with ancient, leather-bound books and rolled parchments, I pulled down a dusty red leather folder from the top of the teetering pile of papers. Untying the red ribbon that bound the folder, I opened it to discover several time-mottled parchments inside. Gingerly, I picked up the brittle document. The manuscript had torn edges and gaping holes in the middle, where a binding ribbon must have once held the document together. The medieval calligraphy looked convoluted, almost foreign, like something one would find in the Library of the Indies, in Seville, were one searching for treasure manifests of galleons sunk in the Spanish Main. I was looking at the first and last pages of a legal document.

After briefly studying the document, I was able to decipher some of the cryptic abbreviations and shorthand flourishes of the ancient handwriting. Though garbled and mutilated, I managed to decipher the first paragraph. It read:

"Don Carlos[116], by divine clemency, Holy Roman Empe(ror)..King of Germany, son, by the same grace of God, of Doña Juana and Felipe, King of Castile, Toledo, Seville, Jerusalem, Granada, the Mallorcas and the Menorcas, Sardinia, Murcia and Jaen, the Algarbes, Algeciras, the Indies Islands of firm land in the sea of the Caribbean,..."

---

[116] Holy Roman Emperor Charles V of Germany, named Charles I of Spain

The familiar grandiloquent preamble hinted at the authenticity of the document, most Royal Court lawsuits of the time starting the same long-winded way. The document proceeded to list the different palaces of Agorreta in Navarre and Labourd, seven in all, describing their individual coats of arms in painstaking detail. I was intrigued by the family title of '*Cabo de Armeria*,' which, I later learned, was a special title of nobility within the Kingdom of Navarre, given to palaces considered the source of lineage, with their own Heraldic Shield and with, among other prerogatives, the right to attend sessions of the Royal Court. Other titles listed were those of Majordomo and Royal Cupbearer, confirming a family tradition that an Agorreta had once hosted a King of Navarre in one of his palaces. Also cited were such privileges as the 'right to walk with kings, live in royal residences, and attend royal councils and coronations.'

Skipping to one of the middle pages, I came across a quaint segment, which read:

"The Palace and House of Agorreta, the principal head of so many noble and illustrious palaces of this Kingdom, has, from time immemorial to this day, possessed and owned the palaces of Azcayn, in the land of Labourd, Kingdom of France, diocese of Bayonne, known by the name of Azcayn Nansegna and by other names, as well as other manors and palaces in Narbart and Gaztelu and Santesteban de Lerín. It has had, and still has, many of its own servants and vassals who, every year owe the lords of the palace vassalage money or wheat, honey, apples, chickens or other services of greater worth in return for defense.."

This feudal exchange of apples for security was the quaintest description of Feudalism I'd ever come across. But what really impressed me was that even as far back as September 1552, the date scribbled just above the document's lacquered seal, the house of Agorreta had already existed 'since time immemorial.'

The housekeeper showed me the oldest part of the house; its kitchen. A huge, beehive-shaped oven, framed by two ancient torch loops, the ceiling directly above them smudged with the smoke of countless firebrands. A huge copper kettle hung from the open hearth. Opposite the oven sat a massive, four-foot tall cylindrical block of solid granite with a deep concavity hollowed out on its top and a small spout sticking out of its bottom. "This was their washbasin," volunteered the housekeeper. "They used ashes for soap," she explained.

It was getting on late afternoon and I had one more place to visit. I thanked the housekeeper, who smiled a toothless grin, happy to see me off. Hopping back in my car, I waved goodbye and headed back up the road toward Burguete. I wondered if anyone else had visited Jaureguizar in the last dozen years and felt a pang of sadness thinking that it would one day just collapse and that that would the end of all that history, the endless brushes with the Celts and the Romans, the Goths, the Moors and the Castilians.

I turned off the main road, midway between the hamlets of Viscarrét and Espinál, proceeding westward down a narrow country lane until the paved road ended abruptly in front of a solitary *caserío* on whose façade a chipped enamel plaque proudly proclaimed this to be Sorogáin, the place of witches. It was the first one-house town I had ever seen. Unhitching a chain on the mountain path, I hopped back in the car and cautiously advanced up a deeply rutted cart path, precariously wending its way up the side of the mountain. Several cows grazed in a slanted meadow above me, their bells echoing peacefully in the narrow valley.

Proceeding up the narrow path, I noticed the road suddenly widening. Looking up I saw what I'd been looking for: there, directly above me, resting on a small promontory

241

overlooking the path, was an odd circular arrangement of grayish, upright stones sticking out of the ground, like a miniature Stonehenge, without lintels. It was the cromlech!

Hopping out of the car, I clambered up the slippery bank, clawing my way up to the center of the *arrespil*[117]. In a circular pattern, some twenty feet in diameter, stood a score of roughly hewn, two-foot tall granite uprights, protruding crookedly from the ground. Circumscribed in the center of the arrangement was an almost imperceptible grassy knoll. The light drizzle and the mists roiling over the weird circle of monoliths gave me a strange feeling that I was not alone.

An inscription on a historic marker by the side of the cromlech proclaimed that the late Iron-Age monument, presumed to be religious in nature, dated two and a half millennia. Being pre-Christian, I surmised that the rites must have been pagan, since sorcery, witchcraft and goat idolatry were prevalent among the mountain Basques, long after the flatland Vascons had been Christianized. In my mind's eye I could see witches dancing on that very cromlech on a moonlit summer solstice. The thought gave me a slight shiver. There was a distinct presence of something unknown in that ghostly place that was making me uncomfortable. I knew it was time to leave.

The sun went down behind the mountains as I slipped and slid down the hill towards the caserío of Sorogáin. As I drove the last few miles north to the Loizu, my grandmother's hotel in Burguete, I tried to recapture the blurring events of that day, from the feat of arms at Roncesvalles to the staggering millennial age of *Jaureguizar*, and finally to the weird, unearthly feel of Sorogáin, each speaking in its own hauntingly quiet way, of the ageless mystery and fleeting splendor that was once Vasconia.

---

[117] Basque for Cromlech